STARTING A BED AND BREAKFAST

Bite Sized Interviews With Successful B&B's on Building a Brand That Lasts

---

JON NELSEN

Life Level Up

Copyright © 2022 by Jon Nelsen

All rights reserved.

No part of this book may be reproduced in any form or by any electronic or mechanical means, including information storage and retrieval systems, without written permission from the author, except for the use of brief quotations in a book review.

Contents

Introduction ix

1. The Katherine Holle House B&B 1
2. Greenbriar Inn 3
3. 1899 Inn Deadwood 6
4. Rabbit Hill Inn 8
5. The Barn B&B Walla Walla 11
6. Brass Lantern Inn 14
7. The Lion and the Rose Bed & Breakfast 17
8. Cameo Heights Mansion 20
9. The Victoria Inn Bed & Breakfast 23
10. Villa Cathedral 25
11. The Inn at Ragged Edge 28
12. BlissWood Bed and Breakfast Ranch 30
13. Connellsville Bed and Breakfast 32
14. Hocking Hills Inn 34
15. Miller Tree Inn 37
16. Ringling House Bed & Breakfast 39
17. Wayne Bed & Breakfast Inn 42
18. Meadows Inn Bed & Breakfast 44
19. The Lincoln Inn & Restaurant At The Covered Bridge ... 46
20. Devonfield Inn 49
21. Beds on Clouds 52
22. Trillium Bed & Breakfast 54
23. Whistling Swan Inn 56
24. The Inn At Five Points 58
25. Shorelands Guest Resort and Cottages 61
26. Hummingbird Inn 65
27. Tinder Guest House 68
28. Weller Haus Bed Breakfast & Event Center 70
29. The Publishing House Bed and Breakfast 73
30. Westbrook Inn Bed and Breakfast 75
31. The Bevin House Bed & Breakfast 78
32. Secrets on Main Bed & Breakfast 80
33. Harvest Barn Inn 83
34. The Grand Kerr House 85
35. The Bear's Den B&B 88
36. The Oaks Bed and Breakfast 90
37. Isabella B&B 92
38. Sage Hill Inn & Spa 94

39. The Dolon House	97
40. Historic Elgin Hotel	99
41. Castle La Crosse Bed and Breakfast	101
42. Dragonfly Ranch	105
43. Ala Kai B&B	107
44. The Inn at Onancock	109
45. Gaslight Inn	111
46. Marias Garden & Inn	114
47. The Baker House Bed & Breakfast	116
48. Ambiance Bed & Breakfast	119
49. The Australian Walkabout Inn B&B	122
50. Chipman Inn	125
51. Bay Tree Manor	128
52. Cedar Grove Inn	131
53. Walnut Canyon Cabins	133
54. Inn at Ellis River	135
55. Equinox Inn at Biscuit Hill	138
56. The Sedgwick House	140
57. Hobble Inn	142
58. Pheasant Field Bed and Breakfast	144
59. The Owl's Perch	147
60. Inn on the River	150
61. Manayunk Chambers Guest House	152
62. 7F Lodge and Events	156
63. Snowgoose Pond Bed & Breakfast	158
64. The Parador Inn	161
65. The Charleston Inn	163
66. Inn Of The Turquoise Bear	166
67. The Yorkshire Inn	169
68. Black Creek Bed and Breakfast	171
69. The Gibson House Inn	173
70. The Dominion House Bed & Breakfast	176
71. Letchworth Farm	178
72. Inn at Glencairn	180
73. Bed and Breakfast at Oliver Phelps	183
74. Black River Inn Bed and Breakfast	186
75. Blue Dragonfly Inn	188
76. Mile Hill B&B	190
77. Oak Creek Lodge	192
78. Purple Martin Inn and Nature Center	194
79. Moonshadow Bed & Breakfast	196
80. Knob Hill Bed & Breakfast	199
81. The Bentley Inn	202
82. Blessings on State Bed & Breakfast	204
83. West Hill House B&B	207
84. Mansion on The Mile B&B	210
85. The Blue Horse Inn	213

86. Oft's Bed and Breakfast	216
87. Cucharas River Bed and Breakfast	218
88. Birchwood Inn	221
89. Nola's Onekama Hideout	224
90. Ashley Manor	228
91. Irving House at Harvard	230
92. The Wayward Traveler's Inn	233
93. Main Street Bed & Breakfast	235
94. Beall Mansion An Elegant Bed & Breakfast Inn	237
95. Serenity Hill Bed and Breakfast	240
96. Sylvan Falls Mill B&B	243
97. Kilgore Mountain Hideaway B&B	245
98. Surf Song Bed & Breakfast	247
99. Hilo Bay Hale Bed and Breakfast	249
100. Avalon Bed & Breakfast	251
101. Brewery Gulch Inn	253
102. Market Street Inn	256
103. Hawaii's Hidden Hideaway Bed & Breakfast	258
104. Maison de Terre	260
105. Maria's Creekside B&B	263
106. Bed and Bagels of Tucson	265
107. Black Bear Inn	267
108. Sweet Dreams B&B	269
109. Whispering Winds Retreat B&B	272
110. Brigitte's Bavarian Bed und Breakfast	274
Final Notes	276
Also by Jon Nelsen	277

SPONSORED CONTENT

SOLAR POWERED ENERGY THEFT

Why Solar?

- Increase your home's value
- Save up to 50% on monthly energy
- Predictable and fixed cost
- Sell home faster
- Protection from inflation
- Peace of mind

FREE DOWNLOAD

JonNelsen.com
• SOLAR CONSULTANT •

Introduction

Bed and Breakfasts are the combination of several great loves of mine. Those loves, being both food and traveling to unknown places. In researching the B&B industry in America, I discovered the kindest collection of individuals who collectively put others first. As you read this and the other books in the America's Best Bed and Breakfast Series, you realize that most of these entrepreneurs don't get into this industry to become wealthy. Instead, they have a genuine love of people despite being part of the competitive travel industry.

These owners offered tips for travelers, advice for future innkeepers, recipes, and their stories. Most of these B&B's are privately owned and operated and depend on their reputation and word of mouth from satisfied customers. I hope this book teaches you something you didn't know about B&B's and inspires you to visit some of these wonderful locations.

Jon Nelsen

ONE

The Katherine Holle House B&B

119 N Church St
Watertown, Wisconsin 53094

∾

Keri K.

WHAT GOT YOU STARTED IN THE B&B INDUSTRY?

I have always dreamed of owning one, even as a small child.

What is your B&B best known for? What is your region known for?

Ours is known for our hospitality - Wisconsin hospitality! (say hi to your ma for me)

What's one piece of advice you would offer to someone looking to open their own B&B?

You have to be a people person, even when you don't feel it!

What was the hardest part about opening?

Getting our name out there and advertising.

With the travel industry so competitive, how are you able to find guests? What is your most successful marketing avenue and why do you think that is?

Word of mouth advertising is starting to be our best marketing. Something wrong? tell us! Something right? Tell a friend (or 5!)

TWO

Greenbriar Inn

315 E Wallace Ave,
Coeur d'Alene, ID 83814

Kris McILvenna

Greenbriar Inn
CATERING AND LODGING

What got you started in the B&B industry?

We were traveling in Europe and enjoyed the experience so much that the following year, when I learned I was pregnant with my second child, I thought I would try a cottage industry business and retire from my job as a stockbroker, to raise both my kids and run a business from home.

What is your B&B best known for? What is your region known for?

Our B and B is well known for its great food an ambiance. We have a dinner restaurant on site as well as a great crafted cocktail bar which our guests seem to really enjoy! We are only four blocks from Lake Coeur d'Alene and only a few short blocks from art galleries, parks, and other restaurants. Our area is known for its beauty, with lakes, rivers, mountains, only a few minutes drive away. We are also only 30 minutes from Spokane, Washington which provides us with additional revenue, as Spokanites love coming over here (North Idaho) to play.

What's one piece of advice you would offer to someone looking to open their own B&B?

I would start small, and pencil in some downtime, even in your busy season. Most B and B's are run by families, as they are 2 to 4 bedrooms. So make sure you don't get burnt out.

What was the hardest part about opening?

When we first opened, in 1985, no one in our area had heard of Bed and Breakfasts. We got some really weird referrals: People thinking we were like a rooming house, or expecting to shower, clean up and leave! Also, we didn't realize that Americans require private baths, and there were none in this Historic House. We ended up adding nine bathrooms.

With the travel industry so competitive, how are you able to find guests? What is your most successful marketing avenue and why do you think that is?

By far and away, booking engines have driven us a LOT of business. Thank you, Internet!

THREE

1899 Inn Deadwood

21 Lincoln Avenue,
Deadwood, South Dakota 57732

~

Nyla Griffith
Innkeeper

WHAT GOT YOU STARTED IN THE B&B INDUSTRY?

We've have a long history in the travel and hospitality industry and so know what we always look for in accommodations. Both my husband Tom and myself love to meet new people and chat. Tom is an author with 80 (mostly travel related to the Black Hills) published books under his belt. He is a professional story-teller and is an expert on Mt Rushmore and the entire Black Hills really. I love to cook and entertain and so it was just a perfect fit for us.

What is your B&B best known for? What is your region known for?

Historical setting with beautiful antiques, great service and fantastic food.

What's one piece of advice you would offer to someone looking to open their own B&B?

Be prepared to work 24/7/365. It takes a lot of energy, attention to detail and you must love serving people.

What was the hardest part about opening?

Everything. Preparing a special place, purchasing all of the soft goods and making sure the bedding is amazing no matter the guest preference for "firm" vs "comfy", organizing all of your reservation software, credit card processing, etc., working with OTAs, hiring great staff... the list goes on and on.

With the travel industry so competitive, how are you able to find guests? What is your most successful marketing avenue and why do you think that is?

The Black Hills is a very popular vacation destination and has been for more than 100 years. Having an amazing website is is the single most important marketing item in the arsenal.

FOUR

Rabbit Hill Inn

48 Lower Waterford Rd
Lower Waterford, Vermont, 05848

∼

Brian & Leslie Mulcahy
Innkeepers

2020 Travel+Leisure #1 Best Resort Hotel in the Northeast

#3 Best Hotel in the USA / #39 Best Hotel in the World

Over the 27 years of our innkeeping life, we've earned several awards and distinctions. Most recently, we are very proud and humbled to have been named #1 Hotel in the Northeast, #3 Hotel in the US, and #39 Hotel in the world in Travel+Leisure Magazine's World's Best Awards. We have appeared on this list several times; but for the past two years, we've taken the #1 spot for the Northeast. What is especially great about this is the company that we're in. This "mom & pop" inn in Lower Waterford, Vermont has taken the lead over properties across the world who charge thousands of dollars per night and have marketing teams that spend more in a day what we might spend in two years.

Rabbit Hill Inn

...a deliciously romantic
Vermont experience!

WHAT GOT YOU STARTED IN THE B&B INDUSTRY?

We started by being guests. Rabbit Hill Inn was the very first inn we visited as a younger married couple. After our experience here, we thought that innkeeping might be something we'd like to do at some future point in time. We didn't know the serendipity that would bring us here so much sooner than expected.

What is your B&B best known for? What is your region known for?

I think that when our guests think of Rabbit Hill Inn, they consider the level of hospitality offered as something they've never experienced before. On top of that, there is a consistency here that our guest can rely on. We strive everyday to provide a magical experience for every guest. Those who come time after time, do so because they always know that an elevated experience consistently awaits them. The area, known as Vermont's Northeast Kingdom, is known for its wide open spaces and pristinely beautiful rural nature. Though rural, there is plenty for people to do. It's a playground!

What's one piece of advice you would offer to someone looking to open their own B&B?

It's not a hobby! It is every aspect of your being. You cannot turn it on and off without being true to yourself. Innkeeping is all that you are – your work, your socialization, your conversation, and for most of us, an investment in our future (retirement).

What was the hardest part about opening?

Can't speak about "opening" as our property has been here since 1795. However, one of the hardest parts of continuing on is making the place your own. At the same time, there is the understanding that the place is NOT your own. We are all just stewards of a piece of history. You could almost say that we don't own an inn but that the inn owns us for piece of our lives. But there are many rewards that come with that.

With the travel industry so competitive, how are you able to find guests? What is your most successful marketing avenue and why do you think that is?

The best way to be successful is to do it right! Sounds simple. But mediocrity just won't cut it. You need to understand your guest and make them want to tell the world about you. Yes, a proper online presence is REQUIRED. But that only helps to get people here. Our job is keep people coming back and sharing their experience with others.

FIVE

The Barn B&B Walla Walla

1624 Stovall Road
Walla Walla, WA 99362

Anand & Naina Rao

After just 9 months in operation we were awarded the TripAdvisor Traveler's Choice Award. We also got 3 Diamonds from AAA.

WHAT GOT YOU STARTED IN THE B&B INDUSTRY?

A lifetime career in hospitality in 8 countries. A love of making people feel special, food and wine.

What is your B&B best known for?

A very high level of personalized service, uncommon amenities like: a private outdoor hot water shower in a private Zen garden; a choice of mattress and a selection of pillows; interesting breakfasts from around the world; a bottle of Walla Walla wine in your suite; complimentary dinner on one night a week. What is your region known for? Walla Walla is the jewel of North Western wine, tucked away in the SE corner of Washington state, boasting amazing wines and over 140 wineries.

What's one piece of advice you would offer to someone looking to open their own B&B?

Make sure you have your own private space built into or apart from the business

What was the hardest part about opening?

We were a new build so all the daily decisions, delays, permits, licenses and details of getting it all together in time for an on-time opening. Getting the lighting right was a huge challenge.

With the travel industry so competitive, how are you able to find guests?

The first year was challenging - we were brand new. But word quickly got around that we offer a new level of service, accommodations and meals in Walla Walla.

What is your most successful marketing avenue and why do you think that is?

TripAdvisor and Google have been great for us. 75% of travelers check TripAdvisor before making their decision. And 88% of internet searches are done on Google. There is nothing more powerful than word of mouth and great reviews on both these sites are crucial. As is referral business and return guests. Once your return guest base is strong, you can reduce the rest of your marketing/advertising costs.

SIX

Brass Lantern Inn

717 Maple Street
Stowe, Vermont

∼

George Lewis

·   Certificate of Excellence, Trip Advisor.com for multiple years of excellent guest review comments

·   2019 Traveler's Choice, Best B&B/Inn in the United States – top 25 B&B in the U.S. from TripAdvisor.com

·   2020 Stowe Business People of the Year Award – recognized by the Stowe Visitor's Center, Stowe Area Association

---

WHAT GOT YOU STARTED IN THE B&B INDUSTRY?

My wife and I met in our mid-20's at a Bed & Breakfast in Stowe, Vermont, while participating with a summer bike tour group. Before we had kids, many of our travels included stays at B&B's. We liked the experience of a home like/unique experience with the opportunity to meet other travelers. After a very fulfilling professional career, me as an architect, and Mary Anne as an occupational therapist, we looked towards the opportunity for a new experience and the potential lifestyle of becoming Innkeepers and the idea of a B&B started to rise to the top of our list of considerations. I ultimately wanted the experience of owning my own business. Reporting to myself (and yes, the guests…) and not to two or three levels of management between myself and the client/guest.

What is your B&B best known for? What is your region known for?

Exceptional personal service, friendly Innkeepers, amazing setting; spectacular views of Mt. Mansfield (highest peak in Vermont). Stowe, Vermont is known as the Ski Capital of the East though just as many guests here during the spring, summer and fall. We are truly a wonderful 4 season destination. We are so very well positioned as an outdoor pursuit type of place or the, grab a drink, and sit on the back porch and soak up the scenery.

What's one piece of advice you would offer to someone looking to open their own B&B?

Wherever you decide to land as Innkeepers, make very certain that it is in a place that you really, really like, because, guess what, you will be there a lot. Our successful four season property has us truly very busy for all but a few weeks in "mud season," after the snow melts, and a couple of weeks during "stick season," after the leaves have fallen and before the snow has begun to transform our location to a winter wonderland. We don't get the chance to venture very far from Stowe on a regular basis, however, this is truly a magical kind of place and we have no regrets, only our lucky stars to thank for this opportunity.

What was the hardest part about opening?

Coordinating and acquiring financing. Convincing commercial bank lenders that our dream is truly viable was truly a challenge. Fortunately, our professional backgrounds and a solid business plan, and equity from selling our former house, provided the financial foundation to get us in the door.

With the travel industry so competitive, how are you able to find guests? What is your most successful marketing avenue and why do you think that is?

Hire a professional photographer, web site developer, and digital ad agency. That investment has been vital to our success in marketing our small business. From there, we are doing our best to maintain brand awareness through various social media channels. As an intimately scaled lodging business, we are able to truly connect to our guests and friends on these channels to stay current with them. And positive guest reviews are absolutely essential to maintaining the health of the business, see awards/recognitions below.

SEVEN

The Lion and the Rose Bed & Breakfast

276 Montford Ave,
Asheville, NC 28801

Karen & Steve Wilson

- Our gardens became a certified wildlife habitat by the National Wildlife Federation.

- We started a fun giving back project called "Inn Support of our Troops". We worked with a non-profit organization, Soldiers Angels, and rallied over 30 other inns to send home baked goodies to soldiers overseas. We plan to make this project an annual event and hope to get more inns to participate.

- In 2021, our B&B was a prize on the epic game show, The Price is Right.

WHAT GOT YOU STARTED IN THE B&B INDUSTRY?

Our very first stay in a B&B was our wedding night. We loved the experience and continued to travel that way from that point forward. Through the years, it became a dream to maybe one day own a B&B. When our jobs became unstable, we decided to make a change, pursue our dream and start a new adventure. In September 2018, we became the proud owners/innkeepers of The Lion and the Rose.

What is your B&B best known for? What is your region known for?

Our B&B is known for being an affordable and comfortable stay that is centrally located in Asheville. We are less than a mile from downtown Asheville where you will find all the great independent shops, restaurants and breweries. We are also only a few miles away from Biltmore Estate which is a huge tourist attraction as it is the largest privately owned home in America. Since we have become the owners of The Lion and the Rose, our B&B has also become known for our beer. Steve has been a home brewer for over 5 years and we decided to incorporate his hobby into the business for everyone to enjoy. Upon check-in, guests receive not only a warm welcome but a complimentary cold pint of beer poured straight from the tap. We also serve beermosas with breakfast on Sunday morning and use the spent grains from the beer in our bread and cookie recipes. The Asheville region is known for the Biltmore Estate, the Blue Ridge Parkway (one of America's most beautiful drives) and it is also known as

Beer City USA for having the most breweries per capita in the U.S. Our region attracts outdoor lovers that are looking for hikes to beautiful mountain views or waterfalls and also adventure lovers looking for an adrenaline rush with ziplining, white water rafting, and rock climbing.

What's one piece of advice you would offer to someone looking to open their own B&B?

If this is your dream, just do it! It's hard work but very rewarding and you will not regret the decision to take on this lifestyle if you enjoy meeting new people and taking on the role of a host/hostess.

What was the hardest part about opening?

We did not start and open a B&B from scratch. Financing made that option impossible for us. The hardest part of our transition was the nerves of serving breakfast to a full table of guests on our first day.

With the travel industry so competitive, how are you able to find guests? What is your most successful marketing avenue and why do you think that is?

Luckily, our B&B was one of the first ones to be established in the Asheville area. It is one of the longest running B&Bs in the area. It has been open since 1985 so we have great word of mouth and we are fortunate to have a lot of return guests. When asked to describe a stay at our B&B, we like to quote William Butler Yeats, "There are no strangers here; only friends you haven't yet met". We do budget for marketing and pay for advertising on certain platforms and use online travel agencies such as Expedia, Booking.com, Airbnb, etc.

EIGHT

Cameo Heights Mansion

1072 Oasis Rd,
Touchet, WA 99360

CAMEO HEIGHTS
MANSION · RESTAURANT · VENUE

We were voted top 10 romantic places to stay in the world (right up there with Paris!) by Bed&Breakfast.com and have also received awards from Opentable for our dining and Trip Advisor for our inn and restaurant.

What got you started in the B&B industry?

Due to financial reversals as we started the development of a 400 acre orchard, we had an empty unfinished large home that was sitting vacant for 10 years in our beautiful orchard/vineyard setting. A banker suggested we look into finishing it as a b&b. We had just sent the last child of our seven children out the door to college and after 37 years of farming, we decided to follow the bankers advice. The rest is history.

What is your B&B best known for?

Romantic stays for couples, good food, good wine, extraordinary service.

What is your region known for?

Wine, good food and history.

What's one piece of advice you would offer to someone looking to open their own B&B?

Do your research. Stay in lots of bed and breakfasts. See what you like and don't like. Talk to owners and talk to the guests who stay in them. If you don't like people and are not willing to go the extra mile to make them happy, it is not a good fit for you.

What was the hardest part about opening?

Finishing up the construction on time for the bookings we had taken and surviving for the first few years until you can get your occupancy up to start paying the bills.

With the travel industry so competitive, how are you able to find guests?

We spent a lot of money on brand awareness in our local area within 100 miles around us, visited county fairs, gave away tons of rooms to well-known people in the community. We attended the annual and state b&b seminars and asked questions about the best people in the industry to get on board for marketing.

What is your most successful marketing avenue and why do you think that is?

The best advertising is doing a great job with the guests who come to our b&b, then they return and tell others—word of mouth! We have each guest fill out a questionnaire when they leave. Sometimes they will write down what they won't tell you to your face. Then, ask every guest what you can do better, be willing to stand behind a satisfaction guarantee even when that means giving money or a gift card to come back free and try it again with the improvements put into place correcting those things that made their stay less than perfect. This guarantees return guests every year and all the friends/family/people they tell about their wonderful experience.

NINE

The Victoria Inn Bed & Breakfast

430 High Street (Rt. 27E)
Hampton, NH 03842

∽

Tracey Dewhurst
Proprietor

"The Seacoast's Finest Lodging & Special Occasion Destination!"

WHAT GOT YOU STARTED IN THE **B&B** INDUSTRY?

I had no interest originally, but saw this property and fell in love with it. Plus there was an event space that offered the potential for more events. It needed renovating but had good bones.

What is your B&B best known for? What is your region known for?

We are located a half mile from the ocean, a short walk, so we are known for great beaches, beautiful coastline and fresh New England seafood. My B&B is best known for uniquely beautiful rooms that are all very different.

What's one piece of advice you would offer to someone looking to open their own B&B?

Hire a staff! Don't try to do it all by yourself!

What was the hardest part about opening?

Getting all the renovations done on time.

With the travel industry so competitive, how are you able to find guests? What is your most successful marketing avenue and why do you think that is?

Our beautiful wedding venue attracts lots of guests to the Inn and I think all the travel booking sites help bring attention to our property, since it is homey and unique among all the chains.

TEN

Villa Cathedral

1202 Williamson Road
Alton, VA 24520

Lucy & Bill

Villa Cathedral

WHAT GOT YOU STARTED IN THE B&B INDUSTRY?

Local family already in the business.

What is your B&B best known for? What is your region known for?

Quiet, comfortable, great breakfast, and convenient to Virginia International Raceway (VIR). Majority of business comes for VIR.

What's one piece of advice you would offer to someone looking to open their own B&B?

Figure out how to automate booking and payment management before starting to take reservations, i.e., don't manage the calendar manually.

What was the hardest part about opening?

Nothing hard about it but it can consume a lot of time. People are fickle.

With the travel industry so competitive, how are you able to find guests? What is your most successful marketing avenue and why do you think that is?

If VIR is open we have business. MANY guests are regulars. Expedia Group has been MUCH more effective than AirBnB has ever been.

ELEVEN

The Inn at Ragged Edge

1090 Ragged Edge Road
Chambersburg, PA 17202

∽

Ken and Barb Kipe

WHAT GOT YOU STARTED IN THE B&B INDUSTRY?

Bought it on a whim - never stayed at a BnB before we purchased it

What is your B&B best known for? What is your region known for?

Historic 17,000 sq ft rail road mansion, stunning architecture and wood work, Steinway grand piano built in 1901 for Harrods of London. Area know for history - Gettysburg, golfing, skiing, antiquing, fishing, hiking.

What's one piece of advice you would offer to someone looking to open their own B&B?

Make it yours - do what works for you. Must enjoy interacting with guests.

What was the hardest part about opening?

Learning the BnB business after having purchased it.

With the travel industry so competitive, how are you able to find guests? What is your most successful marketing avenue and why do you think that is?

We use Facebook and Instagram. Guest reviews - guests like what we do and the way we do it.

TWELVE

BlissWood Bed and Breakfast Ranch

13597 Frantz Road
Cat Spring, TX 78933

∼

Carol Davis

- 2020 Tripadvisor Travelers' Choice Award

- 2018 Certificate of Excellence – Hall of Fame Award Winner in TripAdvisor

- Host of The Bachelor – German Edition

- Southern Living 2016 – Top Historic Destination

WHAT GOT YOU STARTED IN THE B&B INDUSTRY?

Crazy moment! Well, seriously, I wanted to share my property in the countryside with people who needed a getaway from the city life and have some rest and relaxation in a peaceful environment with nature and animals.

What is your B&B best known for?

Individual houses/cabins, outdoor activities, including horseback riding, archery, trapshooting, fishing privileges, Exotic Animal Safari.

What is your region known for?

Not sure. (being close to Houston, other larger cities? Maybe ranching country?)

What's one piece of advice you would offer to someone looking to open their own B&B?

Be ready to work 7 days a week and have conversations with other B&B owners, take an Aspiring Innkeepers Class, read the book "B&B for Dummies"!

What was the hardest part about opening?

Nothing much. Marketing the property, perhaps. Finding good employees.

THIRTEEN

Connellsville Bed and Breakfast

316 W. Crawford Avenue
Connellsville, PA 15425

∽

Lucille King

WHAT GOT YOU STARTED IN THE B&B INDUSTRY?

Returning to the area where my aging mother lived so I may be closer to her. Not ready to retire. Area needed lodging because of the Great Allegheny Passage Trail.

What is your B&B best known for?

It is known for cycling the Great Allegheny Passage and Frank Lloyd Wright's Fallingwater, which is on the International Register.

What's one piece of advice you would offer to someone looking to open their own B&B?

Do plenty of research on the area, potential guests and how to operate a B&B.

What was the hardest part about opening?

Getting all the renovations completed for the opening. As a room was completed, it was rented until renovations were finished.

With the travel industry so competitive, how are you able to find guests?

Referrals, return guests and advertising in the Trailbook.

What is your most successful marketing avenue and why do you think that is?

Referrals and return guests go together because they give us a reputation. One cannot ignore one's reputation. These guests write reviews on Trip-Advisor, Google, Yelp, etc. The other is the Trailbook, which also has a website and is a planning tool for cyclists.

FOURTEEN

Hocking Hills Inn

13984 OH-664 Scenic
Logan, OH 43138

∽

Linda Thomas

Hocking Hills Inn
& Coffee Emporium

WHAT GOT YOU STARTED IN THE B&B INDUSTRY?

We are actually an Inn with a Coffee Emporium located next door. We got started because the House we purchased yearned to be a little Inn

What is your B&B best known for?

A. Charm, cleanliness and location.

What is your region known for?

B. Hocking Hills Region is all about the outdoors, hiking through an amazing backdrop of cave, waterfalls and unique caves.

What's one piece of advice you would offer to someone looking to open their own B&B?

Detail, detail and willingness to go the extra mile to achieve the best atmosphere.

What was the hardest part about opening?

One hurdle after another, getting noticed

With the travel industry so competitive, how are you able to find guests?

We use multiple OTA's Booking, Expedia, Airbnb & VRBO.

What is your most successful marketing avenue and why do you think that is?

Reviews and word of mouth

FIFTEEN

Miller Tree Inn

654 E Division St,
Forks, WA 98331

∼

Susan Brager

WHAT GOT YOU STARTED IN THE B&B INDUSTRY?

I had been teaching elementary school in Forks, where we live and was dissatisfied with my career and how it was going, so had left teaching to try other things. My husband was born and raised in Forks and his parents and a brother still lived in the area, so he wanted to stay here. I was looking to find something that would make me happy and allow us to continue living in Forks. The B&B we eventually bought, came on the market and loving older homes I thought buying it and running the B&B would be a good idea. It took Bill a couple of years to come around to that conclusion, also.

What is your B&B best known for? What is your region known for?

Currently one of the things our B&B is best known for is its relationship to the Twilight series of books and movies. Forks was the setting for the books, though nothing was filmed here. Our Chamber of Commerce designated our inn as the "Cullen" house for tours. We are also known for taking care of fishermen during the fall, spring and winter fishing seasons. People come for both those things and our proximity to Olympic National Park, the Hoh Rainforest in particular. We are also popular with folks traveling to our area for business.

What's one piece of advice you would offer to someone looking to open their own B&B?

To make sure that you have enough rooms to allow you to employ others to work for you, because it is really important for your longevity to not have to do everything yourself and to have time off.

What was the hardest part about opening?

Since ours was an operating B&B when we bought it, I can't really speak to that. One of the hardest things to get used to was making breakfast for paying guests and building our confidence in that area.

With the travel industry so competitive, how are you able to find guests? What is your most successful marketing avenue and why do you think that is?

We find guests through our website. The most of our referrals come from our Chamber of Commerce, our Washington State B&B Association, and other marketing cooperatives that we are associated with.

SIXTEEN

Ringling House Bed & Breakfast

201 8th Street
Baraboo, WI 53913

∼

Julie Hearley & Stuart Koehler

WHAT GOT YOU STARTED IN THE B&B INDUSTRY?

I've always had a dream of living in a big beautiful victorian house that had a bit of local history surrounding it. My fiancé decided to take some aspiring innkeepers classes, to see if it would be something we would like to do, to supplement our income during retirement. we both agreed, that when we retire, we would enjoy hosting other people at our home, and we had the skills to make that happen. I cook, work on marketing via the computer, and am very detail oriented. Stuart is the maintenance man, and has a MBA, so does much of the work with finances. We both love history and architecture, sounded like a good fit.

(Un)fortunately for me, the timeline was moved up because, as a computer programmer, I was getting migraines multiple times a week. As I was getting older they were getting more frequent and worse, so I looked at my fiancé and said, I don't think I can do this anymore, having tried everything I & my doctor & my chiropractor knew of to try to control the migraines. There were always things that helped (food, meditation, chiropractic, etc), but never completely resolved them.

So we decided to start looking for a Bed & Breakfast, and this is the criteria we were looking for:

- Had to have cool architecture

- Had to have at least 5 rooms to rent out so we could make a living at it. Plus one for us, and one for Stuarts (my fiancé) aging mother. All had to have their own attached bathroom or room to add a bathroom.

- Had to have some historic significance in the local area.

There is so much more to this story, but I don't want to go on and on.

What is your B&B best known for? What is your region known for?

Sauk County has a lot of great history behind it, starting with the Ringling Brothers Circus, as well as one of the top state parks in the country: Devils Lake State Park. There are lots of ski hills, hiking, kayaking, biking in the area. It is on the Ice Age Trail, and cross country trail that follows the edge of the last glacier to cover the rest of Wisconsin.

Our B&B was Charles Ringlings first home, one of the five founding members of the Ringling Brothers Circus, which got its start in Baraboo in 1884.

What's one piece of advice you would offer to someone looking to open their own B&B?

If you are running a B&B to make a living, you need at least 5 rooms to rent out, which each need their own private bathroom.

What was the hardest part about opening?

Marketing, getting the word out for travelers.

With the travel industry so competitive, how are you able to find guests? What is your most successful marketing avenue and why do you think that is?

We offer a unique, clean, competitively priced logging option. Your website & your reviews are your key to reservations. Get professional pictures done, and make sure your website comes up on the first page when googled.

SEVENTEEN

Wayne Bed & Breakfast Inn

211 Strafford Avenue
Wayne, PA 19087

∽

Traudi and Bob Thomason
Innkeepers

We were awarded the 2016 Small Business of the Year by the Main Line Chamber of Commerce.

WHAT GOT YOU STARTED IN THE B&B INDUSTRY?

When our youngest daughter went to college, we were not sure what to do with our 7 Bedroom 1885 Victorian.

What is your B&B best known for?

We are the first and only B&B in our Township.

What is your region known for?

Colleges and Universities plus History – Valley Forge and Philadelphia.

What's one piece of advice you would offer to someone looking to open their own B&B?

Make sure your local ordinances allow B&B's.

What was the hardest part about opening?

Getting approval from the Township. It took us two and a half years.

With the travel industry so competitive, how are you able to find guests?

Connecting with local Colleges (Where to Stay!) and Local Businesses.

What is your most successful marketing avenue and why do you think that is?

Being on the College Website. When you visit a college, the second thing that you do is to decide where to stay.

EIGHTEEN

Meadows Inn Bed & Breakfast

212 Pollock St,
New Bern, NC 28560

∼

WHAT GOT YOU STARTED IN THE B&B INDUSTRY?

I love all aspects of entertaining especially creating memorable moments. All the details are important – the décor, food, comfort of the beds and cleanliness of the Inn. Our goal is to help our guests relax and reconnect with their family.

What is your B&B best known for? What is your region known for?

New Bern, NC was the original capital of North Carolina. As such, guests can experience history first-hand!

What's one piece of advice you would offer to someone looking to open their own B&B?

Be prepared to handle the unexpected – from guests with food allergies to COVID19!

What was the hardest part about opening?

We opened during the pandemic so that was the hardest part of our opening. However, we were able to use this time to renovate and update the Meadows Inn. In the end, having this time was a blessing.

With the travel industry so competitive, how are you able to find guests? What is your most successful marketing avenue and why do you think that is?

The internet has "leveled the field" when it comes to finding guests. Most of our Guests find the Meadows Inn online and book their room directly.

NINETEEN

The Lincoln Inn & Restaurant At The Covered Bridge

2709 W. Woodstock Road
Woodstock, Vermont 05091

Mara Mehlman
Proprietor

WHAT GOT YOU STARTED IN THE B&B INDUSTRY?

My partner is a European Michelin Star trained chef and we were passionate about working on a project together. I am American but was living in England when we decided to start the project. We decided to do this project in New England. We model our business as the European "Restaurant with Rooms".

What is your B&B best known for? What is your region known for?

We are known for our restaurant. We are in the quaint village of Woodstock, Vermont

What's one piece of advice you would offer to someone looking to open their own B&B?

Location, Location, location. If you are in a sought-after location, you will already have a high success rate. And be prepared to work nonstop.

What was the hardest part about opening?

Be ready to open before you open. Make sure you have your work organizational systems in place. Make sure your place is spotless. Guests are very concerned with cleanliness.

With the travel industry so competitive, how are you able to find guests? What is your most successful marketing avenue and why do you think that is?

> Bite the bullet. Be willing to pay commissions. Sign up with booking.com and expedia.com. Have a great website with your own reservation system as well. Spend the money and have a professional website.

TWENTY

Devonfield Inn

1800 Devonfield Inn
85 Stockbridge Road Lee, MA 01238

∽

Doug & Jim
Innkeepers

-" Where to Stay in the Berkshires"- The New York Times

- 2020 Traveler's Choice by TripAdvisor

- 2020 Loved by Guests Award by Hotels.com

- 2020 Traveler's Review Award by Booking.com

- 2020 Best of Lee

- 2020 Top Ten Romantic Inns by iLoveInns.com

- 2020 Top Ten Accommodations in the Berkshires by TravelMyth

- Member of Berkshire Elegant Inns

WHAT GOT YOU STARTED IN THE B&B INDUSTRY?

After 30 years in Corporate America it was time to enter chapter 2. We outlined where our passions lied in order to determine which industry to pursue. After evaluating our skill set and interests we realized the hospitality industry was the right path.

What is your B&B best known for? What is your region known for?

Our B&B is located in the heart of the Berkshires where attractions such as Tanglewood Music Festival, Jacobs Pillow Dance, Williamstown Theatre Festival, The Mount, Norman Rockwell Museum, Mass MOCA (to name just a few) entice tourists all summer long. Fall Foliage is a main attraction in the autumn and winter activities at Butternut Ski Lodge, and Jiminy Peak such as skiing, snow shoeing, tubing help ensure occupancy all year long. Our building is 220 years old and in the early 1900's, was the former estate of George Westinghouse, Jr., son of George Westinghouse, the famous inventor. In 1942, when the estate was owned by the John Lloyd family, it hosted Queen Wilhelmina of the Netherlands along with her daughter, Princess Juliana and the two grandchildren, Princesses Beatrix & Irene. They stayed for four months in the summer of 1942. Franklin D. Roosevelt visited the property to meet with the Queen that same summer. The property was converted to a B&B forty years ago and sits on 36 acres of land in the Berkshire Mountains.

What's one piece of advice you would offer to someone looking to open their own B&B?

The best piece of advice we can offer is be prepared for a business that is truly 24/7. We get calls throughout the night from last minute travelers looking for a room. Late check-ins can run from 3pm till 10pm. And most times the day starts before 6am. Also, generally speaking, the less rooms an Inn has, the more hands-on an owner will be with day to day tasks (cooking, housekeeping, laundry, reservations, check-in, check-out, etc.). Lastly, best scenario is one owner who enjoys face to face contact with people and the other owner who enjoys back of the house operations, yet they are able to cover for each other when needed.

What was the hardest part about opening?

> We opened at the end of May which lead immediately into the high season. It was truly a case of baptism by fire. There was no time to ease into the operation. It was like a light switch went off and we were hosting full houses immediately.

With the travel industry so competitive, how are you able to find guests? What is your most successful marketing avenue and why do you think that is?

> I think the smartest marking decision we made was to immediately update our website. When we took over, the site was antiquated, the photos no longer accurately represented the guest rooms and the feel was just tired and old. One of the worse things we felt was to mislead people in regard to the look and furnishing of a room and seeing the disappointment on their faces when they arrived. Find a great design firm along with a high end photographer that specializes in the hospitality industry.

TWENTY-ONE

Beds on Clouds

5320 NY-23,
Windham, NY 12496

~

Rebecca Segerstorm

WHAT GOT YOU STARTED IN THE B&B INDUSTRY?

> By accident because of an accident!

What is your B&B best known for?

> Being No 1 out of 8 BnB's rated by TRIPADVISOR!!!

What is your region known for?

> UPSCALE SKI RESORT

What's one piece of advice you would offer to someone looking to open their own B&B?

> HAVE VERY DEEP POCKETS AND DON:T RUN OUT OF $$$$$$$$
> Deep pockets and willing to work 24/7

What was the hardest part about opening?

> Thats easy you you have enough $$$$$$$$

With the travel industry so competitive, how are you able to find guests? What is your most successful marketing avenue and why do you think that is?

> EXPENSIVE ADVERTISING Cost between 15 and 25% of your bookings!!

TWENTY-TWO

Trillium Bed & Breakfast

5151 River Road, Niagara Falls,
Ontario L2E 3G8 Canada

Brian & Mary

WHAT GOT YOU STARTED IN THE B&B INDUSTRY?

When we had stayed in a local hotel before, we almost always ended up on the same floor as visiting sports teams that were in town. We stayed in an Inn for a milestone birthday and loved how quiet it was. From there we decided that we could do this.

What is your B&B best known for? What is your region known for?

We can accommodate almost everyone, but are the best place for seniors, as there aren't too many stairs as the B&B is a bungalow. We're in Niagara Falls Ontario so I would say that the area is best known for the falls.

What's one piece of advice you would offer to someone looking to open their own B&B?

It's a lot more work than you figured, and it ties you down during the busy season, make sure to take time for yourself and your family.

With the travel industry so competitive, how are you able to find guests? What is your most successful marketing avenue and why do you think that is?

Guests can find us on booking sites, like Expedia, and Booking.com, we do also have our own website, which we can offer a bit lower rates.

TWENTY-THREE

Whistling Swan Inn

110 Main St.
Stanhope, NJ 07874

∽

Rosalind Bruno
Owner/Innkeeper

WHAT GOT YOU STARTED IN THE B&B INDUSTRY?

After we signed our last college tuition check, we wanted to do something else rather than work in a corporate environment.

What is your B&B best known for? What is your region known for?

The Skylands Region of NJ is well known for its outdoor activities. We are located near several state parks, where guests can enjoy hiking, biking, swimming, boating etc. We're very close to two very historic towns, which offer a lot of sight-seeing options.

What's one piece of advice you would offer to someone looking to open their own B&B?

> A B&B is a customer-service oriented business. My advice would be to examine your own personality to determine whether or not you find people fascinating. Do you like helping people or do you find their requests annoying? In order to be successful, you have to like people.

What was the hardest part about opening?

> The hardest part about owning a B&B is managing the business in such a way that guests are happy, but you have time to have a personal life as well.

With the travel industry so competitive, how are you able to find guests? What is your most successful marketing avenue and why do you think that is?

> I would say the two most successful marketing channels are the Internet and word of mouth recommendations. The reasons are clear: we have become dependent upon the online information channel, and people tend to want to stay at a place that has been enjoyed and recommended by friends, family and/or co-workers.

TWENTY-FOUR

The Inn At Five Points

102 Lincoln Ave
Saratoga Springs, NY 12866

~

Eilis & Jim Petrosino

Tripadvisor Certificate of Excellence 2016-2020 (Every year we've been open)

WHAT GOT YOU STARTED IN THE B&B INDUSTRY?

We had rented our home on airbnb and weren't able to live in it as it was so successful. We wanted to find a place we could do something similar but still live on site, kinda the best of both worlds. We moved into our bed and breakfast and began running it, but soon realized living in the place you work is not ideal so we've since moved out and now rent that space to guests as well.

What is your B&B best known for? What is your region known for?

Our B&B is probably best known around our community of Saratoga Springs for the outreach of community we have and the local products we use. I would also say people would commend or know us from our instagram page @theinnatfivepoints . Our city is most known for "Health History + Horses" or that is our motto. We have the oldest race course in America, The Saratoga Race Course + we are noted for our water and springs. Roosevelt begin a spa in Saratoga as he believed in the healing powers of the waters and people still come to the baths (now a spa) to do the same.

What's one piece of advice you would offer to someone looking to open their own B&B?

Honestly, Don't, I truly believe vacation rentals have made it very difficult for someone to run a B&B, do your research, if vacation rentals are banned in your area fantastic, but if not you might find that you'll need to drive down prices to compete with airbnbs which leaves you with little profit. I wonder how long unlicensed vacation rentals will be allowed to run the way the do, but in the meantime I just do not see bed and breakfasts as being sustainable for profit for much longer.

What was the hardest part about opening?

Staffing, it is very hard to find good help which led us to have to do much on our own for months before we could find the right people + turn over is a big thing too.

With the travel industry so competitive, how are you able to find guests? What is your most successful marketing avenue and why do you think that is?

I honestly do not know our most successful marketing avenue as it seems to be from all over. Our website, world of mouth, instagram/facebook, local travel companies we have to pay to list on, etc.

TWENTY-FIVE

Shorelands Guest Resort and Cottages

247 Western Ave
Kennebunk, Maine 04043

∼

Sonja

WHAT GOT YOU STARTED IN THE B&B INDUSTRY?

First, we are not truly a B&B, it just happens that we advertised in every venue offered, back in the day of individual advertising….

Currently, I turned the rentals over to VACASA.com, although we only have 2 cottage rentals left. We started with 36 rooms, most in duplex small cottage buildings.

I took over and made them 34, because 2 units in a small motel building were with shared baths, and since I did not know this, I combined them into one unit each with 2 rooms(one room had a bed, the other had a bed and kitchen…. Very confusing, I made that into living area)

Started out because I THOUGHT I wanted to leave corporate life to have more presence with my children, my body was present but little else…

Plus it was the early 90's, work was scarce after I lost a job with a private company- not good transition from a corporate world.... And the place down the street from us came up for auction via RECOLL.

Took my 401K, savings, etc for down payment and went for it, no idea what I was doing. Fortunately, my husband had a job.

I made muffins first with a mix, the company brought containers of frozen muffin mixes(bought a freezer) Donahue Bros, and gave me a BUNN coffee machine. I bought some of their coffee, but then switched to Gevalia, which I had used personally. Still have that machine 30 years later and use it for charity events or community events like Christmas prelude

Before we gave the rentals to Vacasa last year, 2020, for the last 7-10 years, I ended up with a muffin mix from Sam's club, which had no chemical ingredients, and I used pure organic additions to make them very delicious. We had one family grouping whose children loved the cappuchino kind: krusteau muffin mix, liquid = one cup strong coffee, pure cinnamon powder, organic orange rind, ½ cup dry milk powder, 1/3 c organic soft butter, mix together, then stir in 1-1 ½ c Ghirardelli bitter-sweet chocolate chips. Bake according to mix directions.

When guests became healthier, we added a small fridge with yogurts, and sometimes grapes or mandarins. And we replaced the Bunn with a Keurig.

We are surrounded by Rachel Carson wildlife and a short 10 mins walk to a private beach, that allows public access with little parking. That is /was our draw.

And of course, Maine knows LOBSTERS....

15 years ago I decided to plan my retirement by converting the cottage rooms into 1 and 2 bedroom cottages and sell them as condos, with the house on premises becoming our condo.

Of course that was in 2006, and by 2008 we entered the next crises. We had sold 5 cottages, all were still being rented, with 3 additional ones renovated, and the rest still the older style.

Over the last 3-4 years, we sold these and rebuilt the rest, we currently still own 2, which are for sale.

Over the last 7-10 years, I have seen the large and huge lodging marketing companies to totally take over the rental market. First Worl-dres, hotels.com, then expaedia, booking.com, Airbnb. Without member-ship in them, it would be very difficult to survive.

At first I joined most marketing companies with an online presence, and these then gave way to these behemoths.

Since I came from the computer world, we wrote a property management software in 1994 to run the business (the one's on the market then cost $1000's, which I did not have), and once Maine's mountain, Sugarloaf, had a website, I found a way to also have one. It was written by a guy on monhegan island, with my pictures, and he had a company in Boston to host it on their server. Later I found the company that developed Sugarloaf's wifi network, and we installed one as well.

I mention Sugarloaf a lot because that is where we spent our winters once I became an innkeeper. We had always skied there and after our youngest son showed an interest in ski racing, we resided there for the winter, when the cottages were closed. Our season was mid April to end October.

So your questions…. Before covid, people checked in with us at an office, which also had the 'guest café'. Full payment was at check in, so check out was fairly automatic, guests could just leave their key in the unit and leave, or come say goodbye.

When we gave rentals over to Vacasa, they instituted a keyed entry system, and guests were emailed the key code to obtain the key. This helped a lot once covid hit. Plus I was fortunate with having vacasa, since it would have been extremely difficult to maintain a staff with all the restrictions. Maine opened to some guests in June, more in July and August, then restrictions hit again. And all of this was managed by vacasa.

Vacasa also belongs to the large booking engines, expaedia, booking.com, VRBO, Airbnb, etc. really, without them, innkeepers could not survive.

Before these, I remember days in August when we would have 7-10 rooms open in the mornings, and by 4-5 pm, they were all rented with walk ins. (2018-2019 I could do some of this with booking.com, fill a room/unit last minute) back then, there were also several guests and families, esp Canadian, who would come and stay for 10-14 days. That is now long gone, except for one family group that so far (although they had to cancel 2020 but are booked again for 2021) has come for one week each year since 1994, when the patriarch found us, then brought some family, and over the next years it evolved into a family reunion, with some children now bringing their children…

You can run a 2-3, maybe 4 room B&B by yourself but after that help is needed, my sons worked with me from the time they were 12 and 13, the youngest all the way through his college years.

Help has also changed. I used to hire high school help, and local women. Now that is extremely difficult unless the property is open year round. So early on, I found the J1 visa students from foreign lands, work & travel, which pretty much, until 2020, ran the tourist trade. In the beginning, I found and hired students from England, France, Spain, some of my fellow innkeepers traveled to Ireland. Then when the Eastern European countries opened up (it is an exchange, so the country needs to allow American students to work there as well) most of my summer help came from Poland, Slovakia, Ukraine, Estonia, Belarus, Mongolia, Russia, Turkey, Thailand, China. I am still facebook friends with many of them.

Hours are long, especially if you are small, and/or are open year round. In the beginning, 1992, I got up to do coffee by 6:30 and found myself still doing laundry at 11 pm.

However, my first winter vacation with my sons (husband was working on a ship) in Zell Am See, and visiting with family in Nuernberg over Christmas with the Christmas market, made it worthwhile.

Working a 'regular' job would not give me enough time off. Plus trips to Disney World....

TWENTY-SIX

Hummingbird Inn

14 N Aurora Street
Easton, MD 21601

∼

Eric
Owner

HUMMINGBIRD INN
EST. 2017
EASTON, MARYLAND

- 2018, 2020 Chesapeake Readers Choice Award "Best Bed & Breakfast"

- 2020 Chesapeake Readers Choice Award "Best Breakfast"

- 2020 Chesapeake Readers Choice Runner-Up for "Best Hotel"

- 2018, 2019, 2020 Trip Advisors "Award of Excellence"

- 2017, 2018, 2019, 2020 Booking.com "Travel Review Award"

- 2018, 2019 Yelp "People Love Us Award"

- Some of our other achievements include being the location shoot for a soon-to-be-release feature film on Amazon Prime called "The Detour" about a guy that inherits a B&B in a small town. We also have been selected to be a "Dream Vacation Giveaway" on the national TV game show, "The Price Is Right" (air-date TBD).

What got you started in the B&B industry?

Owning a B&B has been something I had always dreamed about doing. I was extremely selective with regards to location, house size, number of rooms, etc. and spent close to 2 years of focused searching before I found exactly what I was looking for

What is your B&B best known for? What is your region known for?

My B&B (Hummingbird Inn) is known for our breakfast (recently won "Best Breakfast" in the region), our large en-suite rooms, the great property, and the special events we have here both private and public. The region we are located in is known for his historic charm and being surrounded by water.

What's one piece of advice you would offer to someone looking to open their own B&B?

Know what you want and do not compromise. If it doesn't check all your "boxes", keep looking.

What was the hardest part about opening?

Being patient while the business grew. It takes time to get known, found, etc. It will happen, but it doesn't happen overnight. So plan ahead (financially and otherwise) for a slow start.

With the travel industry so competitive, how are you able to find guests? What is your most successful marketing avenue and why do you think that is?

To start, you need to sign-up with all the OTA's and you need to be very active in all forms of social media. As the business grows and your reviews start coming in, your business will grow. We continue to be listed in as many places as possible online. Occasionally we will do some print marketing, but it's low ROI. Know your market, know what your preferred guest demographic is and cater to that. Design your marketing AND your policies/protocols/setup to be attractive to the guests you want to host.

TWENTY-SEVEN

Tinder Guest House

106 S Railroad Ave
Ashland, Virginia 23005

∽

Sharon McKenna

WHAT GOT YOU STARTED IN THE B&B INDUSTRY?

> We enjoy bed and breakfasts and thought it would be fun. The bottom dropped out of our business rental space so we figured we would give it a try. Personally, I prefer a B&B where I meet new people so mine wouldn't really appeal to me as much.

What is your B&B best known for? What is your region known for?

> My B&B is known for my personal touches and suggestions on what to do in the area. We are in a small town much like Petticoat Junction and Mayberry. We have local restaurants that are wonderful, neat shops, a microbrewery, music venues, an Escape Room, Vintage Movie Theatre,

Randolph Macon College, nearby wedding venues and we are only 15 minutes from Richmond or 1 1/2 hours from DC. (And our local restaurants and shops have done an excellent job of keeping folks safe from C-19 obviously some of these venues aren't open at present ie.. the movie theatre, although they showed movies outside until late October)

What's one piece of advice you would offer to someone looking to open their own B&B?

Realize how much work is involved. Honestly, if folks lived in my house with me, I don't think I would enjoy it as much (I just treat them like they are in my house).

What was the hardest part about opening?

The hardest part about opening is getting the word out (however, our assistant town manager booked it for his wedding when the plans came through his office).

With the travel industry so competitive, how are you able to find guests? What is your most successful marketing avenue and why do you think that is?

My most successful marketing is being on airbnb. They give me much of my business. However, many folks have found me by googling and the number of folks booking directly on my website has really increased.

TWENTY-EIGHT

Weller Haus Bed Breakfast & Event Center

319 Poplar St
Bellevue, Kentucky 41073

WHAT GOT YOU STARTED IN THE B&B INDUSTRY?

It was something that was on my bucket list. I had an opportunity to take the leap when the company I had been working for 24 years decided to move their Corporate headquarters from Ft. Lauderdale Florida to Tulsa Oklahoma. It was the right time to start looking for a B&B to purchase. I actually did not start mine from the ground up, but purchased one that had been in existence for 13 years.

What is your B&B best known for? What is your region known for?

We're known for great breakfasts and our gardens. We're an urban bed and breakfast located in a walkable historic neighborhood in a small town--but within one mile of a large city—Cincinnati. So you have the best of both worlds—secluded in a small town feel area but so close to three major sports teams, excellent and extensive dining options, an abundance of festivals and entertainment options, broadway theatre, world class zoo and aquarium and a city with 9 fortune 500 companies headquartered within a mile from us.

What's one piece of advice you would offer to someone looking to open their own B&B?

Whether you are opening a B&B or you're purchasing one that's already in business---if you are there to make money and have it be a profitable business—be in the right location. While every B&B cannot be in a destination location, you either need to be where there is action or you need to create your B&B to actually be the destination. And be sure to have an excess of funds available for keeping your place current, expanding as needed and just everyday maintenance and operations.

What was the hardest part about opening?

I did not open from the ground up, so can't speak to this.

With the travel industry so competitive, how are you able to find guests? What is your most successful marketing avenue and why do you think that is?

Our website brings us substantial traffic as does word of mouth from previous customers. It is almost imperative that you list with one of the OTA's (expedia, booking.com, etc) in order to be seen on the internet and not shoved four pages back in the search engines. While we do a very small piece of business with them, being placed on hotels.com, Travelocity, etc., allows us to be found by those customers that are not aware that we exist. Also, became an expert on your area and talk about things that are going on in your area and at your B&B in blogs, on FB, Pinterest, Twitter and all areas of social media.

TWENTY-NINE

The Publishing House Bed and Breakfast

108 N May St
Chicago, Illinois 60607

❧

Kimberly

We've been featured in Dwell, 25 best hotels in Chicago Conde Nast, Wallpaper, USA Today, Du Jour, CN Traveler, Midwest living publications. Been featured on HGTV "You Live in What?" and The Jam.

WHAT GOT YOU STARTED IN THE B&B INDUSTRY?

Airbnb actually got us started in wanting to own a bed and breakfast. We were hosting people in our spare bedroom in Melbourne Australia. Our house was a converted warehouse and the response people gave inspired us to move to the states (where I am from) and offer a similar experience in a true B&B setting.

What is your B&B best known for? What is your region known for?

> The Publishing House is known for luxury, style, location and exceptional breakfasts. We are in the heart of the West Loop in Chicago which has some of the best restaurants and entertainment that the city has to offer. A true Urban retreat.

What's one piece of advice you would offer to someone looking to open their own B&B?

> It's a lifestyle, not just a business.

With the travel industry so competitive, how are you able to find guests? What is your most successful marketing avenue and why do you think that is?

> Instagram is key for us, social media in general. Many B&B owners lack the effort to engage with social media. You are missing out on a huge travel market, of younger travelers with disposable incomes. People visually search for that unique experience. It is mostly free and only takes a few minutes a day. Also 'free' stays for bloggers, influencers and travel agents. It doesn't cost much and their reach is further than yours.

THIRTY

Westbrook Inn Bed and Breakfast

976 Boston Post Rd
Westbrook, CT 06498

∼

Meri

- 5 star rating on Trip Advisor, Booking.com, Expedia.com, Google and other sites.

- We won the Best of the Shoreline in 2020 and the Trip Advisor travel award for 2020. I am on the Board of Directors for the CT Central Region Tourism board, and the Connecticut Lodging Association.

- I represented B&Bs on the Covid Re-open committee for the lodging.

What got you started in the B&B industry?

I had always planned to have a B&B in retirement. I love entertaining, making a lovely inviting home and general hospitality. I started my career in the restaurant business and then moved into liquor and beer sales for over 20 years. I began to keep my eye on properties and in 2019 decided to quit my job and make my dream come true.

What is your B&B best known for? What is your region known for?

We are on the CT Shoreline, so the entire area is know for quaint villages, our lovely seashore, and beautiful fall foliage. Our town has quite a boating industry and a relaxed vintage vibe. We've only been the owner of our B&B but I'm proud to say we are known for delectable breakfasts, super clean, lovely rooms and warm and friendly hosts.

What's one piece of advice you would offer to someone looking to open their own B&B?

Modern Innkeepers need be as savvy with digital marketing and OTA management, as they are with laundry and baking skills.

What was the hardest part about opening?

We were drinking from a firehose when we started – but what I think we underestimated was navigating our digital footprint – Google my Business accounts and our online reputation.

With the travel industry so competitive, how are you able to find guests? What is your most successful marketing avenue and why do you think that is?

It's all digital and referrals. Reviews are your best marketing tool, and the only way to get positive reviews is to earn them. That requires everyone on staff to do their best every day. OTA's can be Friend or Foe – yes they charge a high commission, but they are how guests shop for lodging and working with them creates great bookings. And of course, your website and SEO is critical. We added a video on our site and we were blown away by the response.

THIRTY-ONE

The Bevin House Bed & Breakfast

26 Barton Hill Rd
East Hampton, CT 06424

∼

Dean

WHAT GOT YOU STARTED IN THE B&B INDUSTRY?

Buying a 1872 Victorian Mansion

What is your B&B best known for? What is your region known for?

The B&B is known for it's history. East Hampton was the bell manufacturing capital of the world in the early 1900's. There were up to 30 manufactures producing cow, teacher, sleigh & many other types of bells. The Bevin bell factory is still running today and is the longest running bell manufacturer in the USA. Bevin Bell produces bells for the Salvation Army, & many other companies. The bell used in the movie It's a Wonderful Life was a Bevin bell. (see attached photo)

What's one piece of advice you would offer to someone looking to open their own B&B?

Advice....be a people person & always have a good attitude. It's a fun job meeting so many diversified people from around the world.

What was the hardest part about opening?

Learning the business, especially if you have never been to a B&B.

With the travel industry so competitive, how are you able to find guests? What is your most successful marketing avenue and why do you think that is?

The Web allows guests to find us. We have people from around the world. From Singapore to Germany, Australia to the Netherlands. When I asked a girl from Thailand how she found us she said I Googled "best bed & breakfast in CT" and she found us.

THIRTY-TWO

Secrets on Main Bed & Breakfast

314 S Main St
Cheboygan, Michigan 49721

∽

Laurie Musclow

WHAT GOT YOU STARTED IN THE **B&B** INDUSTRY?

We are Terry & Laurie Musclow and 41 years ago we were honeymooning on Mackinaw Island, northern Michigan. It was a beautiful sunny fall day and Terry said, "Wouldn't it be something if we lived up here one day?" Laurie replied, "Yeah, and we could run one of these" B&B's were just becoming an alternative to hotels/motels and there were numerous options on the Island. Terry also said that he wanted to dabble in art, and Laurie mentioned that she wanted a Tea Room. They returned to their daily lives, raised a family, climbed the corporate ladder and knew what it was like to have the life sucked out of them trying to meet the demands of corporate America.

And then one day... Just an innocent searching on Zillow opened a door for "dreams to come true." In minutes we were driving 8 hours to see a former B&B, that by the pictures was ready to operate. What we found was a true fixer-upper that had been empty for almost two years. It had been Rooms for Tourists since 1924. After looking the building over with no heat, no water, no electric - we saw potential and purchased the 6 bedroom/6 bathroom opportunity.

Finished in 1982, this Victorian lady with 10 Gables was worth breathing life back into. After 7 months of intense renovations, constant encouragement from residents, and a lot of money we opened for business May 1, 2017. In just a very short time, we were turning potential guests away because of no vacancy and have been blessed with 5-star reviews.

What is your B&B best known for? What is your region known for?

Secrets on Main B&B is within walking convenience to downtown Cheboygan's Breweries, restaurants, shops, marinas and the Opera House. Many visitors to our area take advantage of the miles of trails - quite possibly more trails than anywhere in the United States.

Easy day trips from our location include the Mackinaw Bridge, Mackinaw Island, Michigan's top two most iconic restaurants - Hack-Ma-Tack and Leggs Inn,Tunnel of Trees, the Soo Locks, Tahquamenon Falls, Ocqueoc Falls, and the beauty of northern Michigan.

Northern Michigan has the longest inland waterway in the state. Mackinaw Bridge and Mackinaw Island are the Number 1 vacation destinations in the state - drawing over a million visitors every year.

What's one piece of advice you would offer to someone looking to open their own B&B?

Our guests are who we strive to please and we are highly rewarded by their having a great time on their much-needed vacation. We try to treat everyone like Royalty. If you love what you do, the work is very satisfying.

What was the hardest part about opening?

Choosing our software; tourism partners and building our website.

With the travel industry so competitive, how are you able to find guests?

Having a location near a tourist destination; We belong to our local Chamber of Commerce which promotes local businesses to tourists; We printed Rack Cards and have them placed in Michigan rest areas; Google Search leads guests right to our door; Our website is full of helpful information; We are published in the "Cheboygan Today" - 10,000 circulation; Expedia.com and Word of Mouth - the best advertising!

What is your most successful marketing avenue and why do you think that is?

Expedia - and Reviews. So important. We are in a world where another person's experience highly influences our decision to visit the location - or not.

THIRTY-THREE

Harvest Barn Inn

16 Webb Terrace #3157
Bellows Falls, VT 05101

∽

Rich & Ellen

WHAT GOT YOU STARTED IN THE B&B INDUSTRY?

When my wife and I (Ellen & Richard Sager) got married 35 years ago, we planned out our dream list for the rest of our lives, sort of like a bucket list. We thought it would be fun to own a B&B towards our retirement age. We purchased the Inn July 2017 and it has been a dream come true.

What is your B&B best known for?

We have spectacular views of the Connecticut River. During the warmer seasons, guests sit on our front porch and watch boaters, kayakers, and water-skiers on the River.

What is your region known for?

We have a lot of antique stores, the Vermont Country Store and great restaurants.

What's one piece of advice you would offer to someone looking to open their own B&B?

1) You must truly enjoy people, even if it requires giving up some of your private time.

2) Able to do light maintenance yourself.

What was the hardest part about opening?

Dealing with password changes/Website change overs etc.

With the travel industry so competitive, how are you able to find guests?

We are fortunate to take advantage of social media like Facebook and Instagram, plus it is all free. We spend nothing on advertising except printing brochures.

What is your most successful marketing avenue and why do you think that is?

Again, Facebook and Instagram. We invite guests to each platform and periodically post pictures to keep their interest going. We make each guest experience so nice that they will come again and again and bring their friends.

THIRTY-FOUR

The Grand Kerr House

17777 Beaver St
Grand Rapids, OH 43522

Bob & Cathy Trame

WHAT GOT YOU STARTED IN THE B&B INDUSTRY?

Cathy had been dreaming about owning a B&B for some time - thinking it would be a wonderful way to meet people, earn some extra income in retirement and allow them to live in a home they could not otherwise afford. When Cathy and Bob were living in Wisconsin they attended several B&B training sessions (Wisconsin has a wonderful B&B organization) and looked at several places for sale. However, after having both knees replaced and moving back to Ohio to be near family and friends, Cathy gave up her B&B dream thinking they were getting too old to manage a large house and guests. Shortly after returning to Ohio, The Kerr House went up for auction. We went to the auction out of curiosity and ended up buying the house mostly for sentimental reasons as we had stayed there in the past and were friends with the previous owner. Initially we were unsure of what to do with the house but finally decided to build on its previous history and wonderful reputation.

What is your B&B best known for? What is your region known for?

We are best known as a Romantic Getaway Spot and for offering on-site spa services. The Grand Kerr House was nominated for Toledo's most romantic getaway in 2020 and the spa services were featured in Ohio Magazine. Located in Grand Rapids, OH, this small town is known for its history, shopping, dining and area parks offering kayaking, bicycling and hiking.

What's one piece of advice you would offer to someone looking to open their own B&B?

Do not do it for the love of money (you will never get rich) but for the love of the house and your desire to share it with your guests. We have known single people who have managed B&B's but partnering up with someone to share the work load is a blessing.

What was the hardest part about opening?

Identifying our target market. We were able to build on the reputation of the previous Kerr House but had to differentiate ourselves and establish our own reputation (need to get those 5 star ratings!).

With the travel industry so competitive, how are you able to find guests? What is your most successful marketing avenue and why do you think that is?

It's all about the internet and word of mouth. We tried local written advertising and tracked how guests heard of us. Half were through internet searches and half through word of mouth, few were through written advertising. Google Ads and Facebook Ads reach a lot of people.

THIRTY-FIVE

The Bear's Den B&B

864 Driftwood
Page, Arizona 86040

∼

Bubba & Deb-b Ketchersid

WHAT GOT YOU STARTED IN THE **B&B** INDUSTRY?

We worked in the travel industry for 35 years. When we retired, we started our B&B because we live in the middle of the Grand Circle and have about 4.5 million guests a year.

What is your B&B best known for? What is your region known for?

Guest service! We work hard both before and while our guests are here to provide the best customer service possible. We live in the heart of the Grand Circle with 16 National Parks, National Monuments and State parks surrounding us. Antelope Canyon, Horseshoe Bend and Lake Powell only 15 minutes from our B&B and other National Parks like the

Grand Canyon, Bryce and Zion Canyons and Monument Valley less than 2 hours away.

What's one piece of advice you would offer to someone looking to open their own B&B?

It is a big commitment both time and money. You are pretty much married to it 7 days a week. Before you go into the business, make sure you find a B&B and asked to work with or at least ask the inn keeper what it is.

What was the hardest part about opening?

As with any business the hardest thing is just getting it open for guests the way they want it. Making sure you put yourself in the customers shoes and what you would like when you travel.

With the travel industry so competitive, how are you able to find guests?

Booking.com, Expedia, TripAdvisor and AIRBNB are all good platforms however the most important thing is to make sure you are up with the trends, every year things change. What worked great last year may be something totally different this year. What is your most successful marketing avenue and why do you think that is? The most successful is being able to change with what avenue guests are viewing.

THIRTY-SIX

The Oaks Bed and Breakfast

516 Oak Avenue
Sulphur Springs, TX 75482

Allison Libby-Thesing

What got you started in the B&B industry?

We had purchased a smaller home in our community and were in the process of remodeling it as a rental property. The real estate agent who sold us the house liked the work we were doing no asked my husband if he wanted to see a house he was about to list. He stopped by the house and saw the potential for a future business. A bed and breakfast plus event center in town.

What is your B&B best known for? What is your region known for?

Our delicious food, breakfast or catering. Our region is known for our glass bathrooms.

What's one piece of advice you would offer to someone looking to open their own B&B?

Have a marketing plan in place.

What was the hardest part about opening?

The hardest part was probably remodeling the house. We wanted to make sure to keep the history of the house while giving it an updated feel.

With the travel industry so competitive, how are you able to find guests? What is your most successful marketing avenue and why do you think that is?

A lot of guests find us because of positive guest reviews. We strive to make each visit amazing which leads people to return again and/or leave great reviews. I haven't found the best marketing Avenue yet.

THIRTY-SEVEN

Isabella B&B

1009 Church Street
Port Gibson, MS 39150

∽

Bobbye Pinnix

WHAT GOT YOU STARTED IN THE B&B INDUSTRY?

> Desire to continue working during retirement years.

What is your B&B best known for? What is your region known for?

> Southern hospitality with "home away from home" atmosphere. Civil War History and Game Hunting

What's one piece of advice you would offer to someone looking to open their own B&B?

It is a full-time job and you definitely need to be a people person.

What was the hardest part about opening?

The logistics of getting your on-line website calendar set up to schedule reservations.

With the travel industry so competitive, how are you able to find guests? What is your most successful marketing avenue and why do you think that is?

Having a good website set up for on-line reservations and mobile device friendly. We are also in close proximity to The Natchez Trace Parkway so therefore we made sure that all visitor centers on the Parkway knew about our establishment. Word of Mouth is still and always will be the best advertisement you will ever have. Becoming a destination for guests is important!

THIRTY-EIGHT

Sage Hill Inn & Spa

4444 Ranch to Market Rd 150
Kyle, Texas 78640

∽

Brad Burkhart
General Manager

We have the certificate of excellence from trip advisor for the past 4 years running. We also have recognition of excellence from hotels combined.

What got you started in the B&B industry?

I fell into the B&B industry by accident. I started out working for some of the larger hotels brands like Omni Hotels.

What is your B&B best known for? What is your region known for?

We are in the Texas Hill Country. We are known for our breathtaking views and sunsets. Locally there are a lot of wine vineyards.

What's one piece of advice you would offer to someone looking to open their own B&B?

Make sure that you work the industry for a few years before attempting to start your own B&B.

What was the hardest part about opening?

Learning the many skills in order to run each aspect of a B&B. You need kitchen skills, accounting skills, people skills, software knowledge, housekeeping skills, maintenance skills, Gardening skills, wildlife wrangling skills, and so many more.

With the travel industry so competitive, how are you able to find guests?

What is your most successful marketing avenue and why do you think that is? Repeat Customers are the #1 market. For new customers google ads and ranking is the way to go.

THIRTY-NINE

The Dolon House

5 W Broadway
Jim Thorpe, PA 18229

∽

Michael Rivkin

WHAT GOT YOU STARTED IN THE B&B INDUSTRY?

Jeffri and I come from hospitality and culinary arts, and had done inn-sitting , so this was a perfect 'semi-retirement' choice.

What is your B&B best known for? What is your region known for?

Ours is a landmark historic millionaire's mansion, filled with extensive collections of art and antiques. Our farm-to-table, 3 course breakfast is for sure a signature. And our town is known for its historic attractions, cool shops and pubs, scenic railroad and a variety of outdoor activities from hiking and bilking to white water rafting and horseback riding.

What's one piece of advice you would offer to someone looking to open their own B&B?

For sure an internship, a stint as an innkeeper or inn-sitter first!

What was the hardest part about opening?

Honestly, there really is not anything to say here.... We really have had a smooth time of it!

With the travel industry so competitive, how are you able to find guests? What is your most successful marketing avenue and why do you think that is?

Word of mouth among previous guests and locals, on-line reviews like TripAdvisor, careful use of OTA's, good utilization of regional TPA tools. TripAdvisor is for sure our top source, followed by Google. And community involvement and visibility is imperative... being active in the Chamber of Commerce, Visitor's Bureau, civic organizations...

FORTY

Historic Elgin Hotel

115 N Third
Marion, KS 66861

~

Tammy

WHAT GOT YOU STARTED IN THE B&B INDUSTRY?

An 1886 hotel came up for sale in our community. At the time, I was running my own travel agency and had always dreamed of owning my own product in the tourism industry. I decided to go look at the fully renovated hotel that is listed on the National Register of Historic Places, and I fell in love with the place. It wasn't currently open to the public and all I could think about was how this treasure needed to be shared. After a year of planning and crunching numbers, my husband and o made an offer on the property. We closed on the property 6 months later and have been running the Historic Elgin Hotel for the past 4 years.

What is your B&B best known for? What is your region known for?

Blending the nostalgia of the past with the luxuries of today. It's historic nature and elegance and the fact that we are location in a small historic town just an hour from Wichita and two hours from Kansas City, draws people to us. Our area is known as the Flint Hills and for the Tallgrass Prairie National Preserve.

What's one piece of advice you would offer to someone looking to open their own B&B?

Be realistic with yourself and your numbers and recognize that you cannot do everything in the business. Outsource and hire employees to keep yourself focused on growing the business. Do your due diligence and know what you are getting yourself into! Talk to other B&B owners!!!

What was the hardest part about opening?

Being open and doing construction at the same time. Also, building a good team that values the place like you do.

With the travel industry so competitive, how are you able to find guests? What is your most successful marketing avenue and why do you think that is?

Our most successful marketing has been online with Google Ads and Facebook and Instagram postings.

FORTY-ONE

Castle La Crosse Bed and Breakfast

1419 Cass St
La Crosse, WI 54601

~

Billy Bergeron & Brandon Rigger

WHAT GOT YOU STARTED IN THE B&B INDUSTRY?

What got us started was primarily the house, which we found online on Facebook on a page called "for the love of old houses". The Castle had been on the market for over a year and people were starting to wonder what may happen to the iconic home. It is difficult to sell a home in the $1M price range in a small town. The posting on facebook was getting a lot of attention and comments, so it kept popping up. We were living in Houston, Texas at the time and I looked at the photos a few times, then told my partner I'd found the house. He reminded me we were not house shopping at the time and we had never been to La Crosse, WI. We have family in Minneapolis, just two hours away, so on a trip to visit them we went to La Crosse to see the house. It didn't take long to decide it was perfect for a B&B, the house had four bedrooms with private baths all on one floor, an amazing kitchen and a parking lot! At one point the Castle was owned by the Diocese of La Crosse and was the home of the Bishop, they put in the parking area. We made an offer that was accepted in a day, then the fun began. Moving across country and starting a business is a leap of faith. We don't regret it at all, have made a few minor mistakes and definitely plan to continue.

What is your B&B best known for? What is your region known for?

Our home was known as the Castle on Cass for decades, but who knows Cass Street in La Crosse, WI. We changed the name to Castle La Crosse in 2017. Our home is known as a grand 19th century home, a landmark and one of the few surviving mansions of that time in La Crosse. Architecturally, it's worth studying and the most photographed home in the region. Also (refer to item #1) the story on facebook about the house got the most likes and shares of any story that site has run, so they ran it again and one more time when we opened the B&B. The region is known for outdoor activities, the bluff region is famous for hiking, there are trails for hiking and biking all around us. Near La Crosse is Sparta, WI, the bicycle capital with miles of bike trails and tunnels that were once train tracks. We are right on the Mississippi River, so boating and anything on the water. One big event in the winter is called Rotary Lights, put on by the Rotary Club, it's a very big event with thousands of visitors. We are becoming known for our food, there are a few outstanding restaurants, the type you would find in major cities.

La Crosse is "the Friendliest Midwest City" and the people are really nice here, it's a healthy place to live. We have three universities in La Crosse, including the well known University of Wisconsin-La Crosse. We are also just 40 minutes from Ft. McCoy Army Base and have quite a few enlisted people as guests.

What's one piece of advice you would offer to someone looking to open their own B&B?

Advice = Do It! It's a wonderful life, if it fits your personality. I read you should not open a B&B if you need a lot of personal space or you have a problem with people using your things. If it is accessible for the guests, I don't have a problem with them using it, moving it or even breaking it as accidents do happen. It's a profitable, interesting business! If they have gotten so far as to ask a B&B owner if they should open one of their own, they have already decided to do it, they just need a little push. Join clubs, organizations and chat with other innkeepers. Also, important advice, have an Exit Plan. Decide how long you want to run your B&B, what will happen next. Will your children continue the business, will you close and simply enjoy living in your home, will you sell the house or try to sell it as an ongoing business?

What was the hardest part about opening?

The hardest part of opening is the lack of information from the City, County and Organizations. Finding the right permit to apply for is not easy, typically the Chamber of Commerce can help. The city may not have issued a B&B permit in years, also chat with the City Administrator if they have one or the City Planner. "Running a Bed & Breakfast for Dummies", buy it.

With the travel industry so competitive, how are you able to find guests? What is your most successful marketing avenue and why do you think that is?

Travel is competitive, you can have the most amazing gilded-age mansion with Tiffany windows, but if it is not in or near a destination, the guests will not come. Do not try to make it something it is not. If you have the house but not the market, you can create a spa or retreat if you can spend a lot more money, then spend it again on advertising your retreat. We chose our home because the house is amazing, it's the most intact 19th century mansion in the region. But the region is vibrant on it's own, we are halfway between two major cities, Minneapolis, MN and Madison, WI. Being two hours from each of those and just four hours from Chicago, plus we are on the way to many places, so travelers find us.

We have had good luck with Facebook ads and TripAdvisor reviews. Last year we won an award from Booking.com, one of our booking services. This year we won "Travelers Choice" from TripAdvisor. Take those awards and blast them far and wide, third party recognition is a powerful thing. Repost on Facebook monthly, add it to a blog and remind each guest that stays with you.

FORTY-TWO

Dragonfly Ranch

84-5146 Keala O Keawe Rd
Captain Cook, Hawaii 96704

~

Barbara Moore
Soul Proprietor

WHAT GOT YOU STARTED IN THE B&B INDUSTRY?

It was my desire, after a vision quest in Egypt in 1980, to provide a place of healing and growth. Gradually, as my house evolved into five bedrooms, I decided to make it into a bed-and-breakfast.

What is your B&B best known for? What is your region known for?

The Dragonfly Ranch is a uniquely chic Eco boutique. Many people think it is like a Swiss family Robinson treehouse with indoor outdoor living. One guest said, "it's like living inside the outdoors" with year around temperature of about 72 degrees. Swimming with the dolphins who like to be with respectful snorkelers, is one of the most exciting activities in three nearby pristine bays. Not too far away, (and not too close!) is an active volcano. Seeing the stars from Mauna Kea is also exciting.

What's one piece of advice you would offer to someone looking to open their own B&B?

If you are looking to have a lifestyle that includes hosting interesting people, and you don't mind giving up your privacy and working long hours for very little money, by all means, open a B&B!

What was the hardest part about opening?

Getting permitted by the state of Hawaii.

With the travel industry so competitive, how are you able to find guests? What is your most successful marketing avenue and why do you think that is?

Now that I have had the Dragonfly Ranch since 1974, word of mouth and returning guests works well. Multiple internet sources, especially AirB&B, is most effective.

FORTY-THREE

Ala Kai B&B

15 - 782 Paradise Ala Kai
Keaau, HI 96749

∾

Erich Zipse & Suzy Chaffee

WHAT GOT YOU STARTED IN THE B&B INDUSTRY?

I was a real estate re-developer of apartment communities in California and wanted to make a big lifestyle changes. My fiancé and I decided to buy a B&B in Hawaii and were surprised at how inexpensive the wonder beach house with a pool was! It is our way to live in an amazing house and have a great business.

What is your B&B best known for? What is your region known for?

Our B&B is known for a wonderful, remote and quiet repast to stay and relax and explore East Hawaii's Big Island. Our region is known for great coffee, volcanoes, whale watching, tropical rainforest.

What was the hardest part about opening?

One challenge has been working with Expedia. It seems that they have lost so much staff due to COVID that we never got to talk to an account manager to discuss the contract. After three months, we are finally up and running on Expedia. COVID is also a problem getting travelers here.

FORTY-FOUR

The Inn at Onancock

30 North St
Onancock, Virginia 23417

~

Kim
Owner/Innkeeper

- Top 25 Bed and Breakfast in North America by BedandBreakfast.com in 2017.

- We have a 9.9 rating on Booking.com.

- We have received a 5-star Certificate of Excellence every year from TripAdvisor and were named to their top 10% of properties reviewed worldwide in 2020.

- We also were named Best Bed & Breakfast in the 2020 Locals Choice awards.

WHAT GOT YOU STARTED IN THE B&B INDUSTRY?

We purchased a property that had been running as a B&B for 9 years.

What is your B&B best known for? What is your region known for?

The Inn at Onancock is best known for our Wine Down Hour, the butler tray outside your door in the morning, our delicious breakfasts, our dog (Dante) and we the hosts. The Eastern Shore is known for its waterfront beauty, small, friendly hometown feel, seafood, and outdoor lifestyle.

What's one piece of advice you would offer to someone looking to open their own B&B?

Interview other B&B owners and/or shadow a B&B owner for a week during the busiest season.

What was the hardest part about opening?

Keeping reliable housekeeping staff.

With the travel industry so competitive, how are you able to find guests? What is your most successful marketing avenue and why do you think that is?

Our most successful marketing comes through Google, TripAdvisor and our Constant Contact newsletter. Reviews are incredibly important.

FORTY-FIVE

Gaslight Inn

1727 15th Ave
Seattle, WA 98122

~

Bennett

WHAT GOT YOU STARTED IN THE B&B INDUSTRY?

After grad school I moved to Seattle from the Wisconsin, and immediately fell in love with this beautiful coastal city, I love architecture so I started buying and renovating early 1900 homes. I came across the Gaslight in poor repair and was being used because of its size (7,000 sq. feet) as a rooming house. It had all of its original moldings, light fixtures, hardware, and bevelled and stained glass windows but was in extreme need of all its major guts. Of course I fell in love with it and immediately set out to buy it. To answer the 1st question, it was because I found myself over my head financially and I needed to be creative in away that I could keep this gem and restore it but still be able to afford to live there. Goal, After restoration a 8 room B&B in a residential neighborhood that was admired and sought after by tourists and visiting family members but zoned so there were NO hotels.

What is your B&B best known for? What is your region known for?

The Gaslight-Inn is famous in Seattle, for its Historic Landmark status: It was built by the Singerman family who were a family that built the 1st Department Store in downtown Seattle in 1895. Then after my restoration we opened in 1980 and were immediately a success. We were instrumental in the late 80's and 90's helping our Community with the aids crisis, which further built its historical significance to the city and finally the architecture is a perfect 4 square design.

The Pacific Northwest is known for its natural beauty, waterways, Puget sound, massive islands and ferry systems, Proximity to major west coast mountains. Hiking, skiing and all outside activities. Seattle know for its art and music scene, major tech companies, Amazon, Microsoft, Boeing, Starbucks, REI, and on and on! As you can see, the melting pot of innovative and energetic people!

What's one piece of advice you would offer to someone looking to open their own B&B?

That is impossible, since it is a combination of many strong traits that all must be present for the business to work. You need to like and enjoy people, a tolerance for time and communication, the type of person who loves to please and accommodate, and the list goes no and on.

What was the hardest part about opening?

I believe it was the fact that I would from that point on be living communally and I had always been a loner. I was not sure that I could handle that, but it worked out great and I believe after these 40 years I could no longer live in a structure where I was the only one.

With the travel industry so competitive, how are you able to find guests? What is your most successful marketing avenue and why do you think that is?

Another question of yours Jon that really cant be answered in "ones". When I began it was all written travel books that recommended you and gave you ratings, I was always at the top. Next was written travel books but where you paid to be in them so you could write your own narrative, Then came websites so I morphed and paid for the best writer, photographer, and web designer I could. Still staying the most popular B&B in Seattle. Then came 3rd party bookings and AirB&B. That is where we are now. Here is my personal spin on this……and this is not me getting older or, tired of my industry, or cynical, but B&B's are getting less and less popular with a much smaller crowd then in past years. More and more people are $ driven then they are by visuals, history, or uniqueness and that is just a realty. I still love this business, I still Love people, and I still offer a great deal for what my guests receive but we are now competing with many more 1,000's of available rooms a night in our large urban areas like Seattle. I am still on the top, because of the house and its history, the heated pool that is unique here in Seattle, the location on a exciting popular neighborhood, Capitol Hill, and my willingness to play the game with 3rd party booking's and reduce my rates to be competitive.

FORTY-SIX

Marias Garden & Inn

42 Independence Street
Berkeley Springs, WV 25411

∼

Curtis

WHAT GOT YOU STARTED IN THE B&B INDUSTRY?

We got started in the B&B aspect of our business from our restaurant back in 1983. People would come and eat and a common question was where is a good place to stay. It was natural for us, but only having a few rooms it was hard to market cost effective. you have to be committed just like any service business. NO ONE will run or work your inn like yourself.

We have since closed our restaurant after deaths in the family and illnesses. But I am 66 years old and still love fixing breakfast for my guests. I am the local tour guide for them. I am also the bomb at breakfast. Just keep some pancake mix around, some eggs, frozen green peppers, some small cans of mushrooms, an onion, milk juice, and you have the ingredients for a plethora of breakfast treat. I always add french vanilla pancake mix to my pancakes. UMMM. makes great waffles too.

I believe a TRUE B&B is what is needed in America again. Small family business dedicated to taking care of people. Let them have an experience.

With the travel industry so competitive, how are you able to find guests? What is your most successful marketing avenue and why do you think that is?

Booking.com, expedia.com, & airbnb have saved the day for us. The commission charged is well worth the return versus advertising elsewhere.

FORTY-SEVEN

The Baker House Bed & Breakfast

65 W Market St
Rhinebeck, NY 12572

∾

Sandra & George Baker

WHAT GOT YOU STARTED IN THE **B&B** INDUSTRY?

I have always been attracted to independently operated establishments be they bookstores, record stores, or antique shops. Unlike the monoculture of corporate chains, the appearance and business structure of independent business's cannot help but reflect the temperament, eccentricities, and tastes of their owner. I consider myself to be an antiquarian and old house enthusiast and innkeeping allows one to give visual expression to the pursuit of beauty, be it through decorating, cooking, or garden design in an intimate and meaningful way. As one apathetic about capitalism, I believe there are few better paths to escape a corporate office fate and foster the noble pursuits of historic preservation and hospitality than by running a B&B.

What is your B&B best known for?

We offer a complimentary Happy Hour daily where our guests have the opportunity to congregate for socializing with us and each other. We offer snacks, wine, beer, and a craft cocktail of the day. As we often post an image of the cocktail on Instagram, it gets the word out.

What is your region known for?

The Hudson Valley's awe-inspiring natural scenery attracted America's foremost landscape painters in the nineteenth century, helping to establish the area as an appropriate setting for some of the grandest and most ambitious architectural creations of the Gilded Age. Thousands of people come to tour the estates of the Vanderbilt, Roosevelt, Livingston, Morse, and Mills families, as well as the studios of important artists such as Thomas Cole and Frederick Church.

What's one piece of advice you would give someone looking to open their own B&B?

If you are going to do your own housekeeping, you can't have an aversion to human hair. Also, it helps if a couple enjoy spending great amounts of time together working as a team.

What was the hardest part about opening?

To afford to buy a property large enough to accommodate multiple guest rooms in an affluent tourist town, we had no choice but to purchase a derelict house that required years of hard labor and marriage threatening stress to make habitable.

How are you able to find guests?

We paid a great price, literally and figuratively, to have a house that is surrounded by woodland but is a mere five-minute walk to over twenty restaurants. We have an unconventional mix of both seclusion and high visibility. As such, our location sells itself and is our greatest asset.

FORTY-EIGHT

Ambiance Bed & Breakfast

774 Lost Mountain Lane
Sequim, WA 98382

Dave and Corinne FitzPatrick

WHAT GOT YOU STARTED IN THE B&B INDUSTRY?

We always loved accommodating people from around the world, especially those who did missionary work and needed a place to rest. We stayed at our B&B the year before we purchased it as part of our 25th wedding anniversary celebration. So when it came up for sale the following year, we decided it was the right timing and we retired from our jobs in corporate life and as medical receptionist, and moved to Sequim which is so beautiful.

What is your B&B best known for?

Our peace and quiet environment, luxurious suites with claw-foot soaking tubs, the breathtaking view from 1900 feet elevation looking over the Strait of Juan de Fuca, Victoria Canada, the San Juan Islands, and Mount Baker.

What is your region known for?

The Olympic Peninsula with multiple National Parks, The Hoh Rain Forest, Hurricane Ridge, numerous beautiful hiking trails, and Kayaking on Lake Crescent and the Strait of Juan de Fuca.

What's one piece of advice you would offer to someone looking to open their own B&B?

Make sure you read all the state, county, and local laws and regulations for Bed & Breakfast, and Health requirements before investing in a B&B property.

What was the hardest part about opening?

Knowing what you want to brand yourself as and getting the materials to support that brand. Also, setting up a web site and trying to decide where and how often to advertise and market.

With the travel industry so competitive, how are you able to find guests?

The #1 key is getting 5-star reviews from Expedia, Trip Advisor, Google, etc. We maintain an Instagram and Facebook account in which we regularly show pictures of our property and the wildlife in the area. The more you post on various sites, the more Google is likely to show your property in the search. We avoid a lot of expensive fees for advertising and rely more on our guests high ratings and word of mouth.

What is your most successful marketing avenue and why do you think that is?

Great pictures, with a presence on Expedia. 50% of our business comes through Expedia.

FORTY-NINE

The Australian Walkabout Inn B&B

837 Village Rd
Lancaster, PA 17602

∽

Lynne & Bob Griffin
Owners

WHAT GOT YOU STARTED IN THE **B&B** INDUSTRY?

Prior to owning a B&B, my husband was in ministry and I was an insurance adjuster. We loved entertaining, cooking, home improvement projects and meeting new people. We seemed to always have something in the works – inside projects in the winter months, something outside during the spring and summer. Every few months we'd have dinner parties at our house of 10-15 people. Bob is really into wine, so he would pair a wine with each course. We'd have a theme and he'd prepare tasting notes and summaries of the wine and its origins. We had thought of 'maybe someday' owning a B&B, but thought it was something you did after you retired from your 'real' job.

Then for his 40th birthday, we planned a dinner at the Inn at Little Washington. At the suggestion of an acquaintance, we booked a weekend at a B&B nearby called the Foster Harris House. Up till that time, we'd only stayed in a couple of B&B's, and all the innkeepers we had met were folks much older than we were. When we got to the Foster Harris House, Diane McPherson greeted us. She wasn't the little old Scottish lady that we had expected, but a lady of 39 with a new baby! We spent the afternoon chatting with Diane and her husband John (who have since sold the Foster Harris House and now own a restaurant in Sperryville, VA called the Three Blacksmiths). After about a year and a half of research and tours, we ended up in Lancaster.

What is your B&B best known for? What is your region known for?

People who have stayed with us probably remember our inn because of its unique name. We are the 3rd innkeepers and the first couple who purchased it in 1986 were Australian. They named it. The 2nd owners kept the name and so we decided to also. Interestingly enough, though, when we bought it the property had nothing Australian about it, other than the name. So we decided that we needed to run with it or do something different. So we re-named 3 of the 5 rooms to Australian wine regions – the Barossa, the Adelaide Hills, and the McLaren Vale. I also put leather boomerang keychains on the room keys and added some native Australian stuffed animals that sit on the bed in each room, along with a few other down-under types of elements. Nothing overboard, just a few fun things.

Our region is most know for the Amish, of course. However, our downtown area has recently been recognized for its excellent restaurants, cafes, boutique shops and craft breweries. Because Lancaster is a very drivable destination for people from many major East Coast cities, we attract some 8.5 million tourist a year. Because of this, Lancaster County has more B&B's than any county other than a couple in California. Pennsylvania also has more than any state other than California.

What's one piece of advice you would offer to someone looking to open their own B&B?

I would recommend joining a local or state B&B association first thing and get yourself connected with a group of like-minded business people in your area. This is not a career that you can do on your own. You need your local and/or state associations for education, advocacy and networking. The cost to join these is usually minimal. You can't look at it as money you're spending to put 'heads in beds', but rather as an investment in you and your business.

Also, do plan for some down time to recharge. You're going to be 'on' 24/7, so plan for some down time. This is not an endeavor for the faint of heart or weak of knee. Ask for help when you need it.

What was the hardest part about opening?

Probably not knowing what to expect. You're dealing with the general public, so anything can happen. You'll fall into a routine soon enough, but make sure you have a plan for emergencies.

With the travel industry so competitive, how are you able to find guests? What is your most successful marketing avenue and why do you think that is?

We are equal-distant between three of our county's largest convention spaces, so (pre-pandemic) I would often find out what groups were hosting conferences, conventions and trade shows and contact their organizers and ask them to put us on their list of alternative lodging. I found that this worked quite well. Since we only have 5 rooms, I'd fill a few of them during the event and often guests would come back either when they returned to that event or when they would come to the area for vacation travel.

Additionally, I find that nurses, police officers and teachers are some of my best referral sources. I ask these guests to take a few of our rack cards and put them in the break room at their job.

FIFTY

Chipman Inn

1233 VT-125
Ripton, VT 05766

Chris Bullock
Innkeeper

- "In Search of the Perfect Vermont Inn," New York Times Travel Section, July 18, 1982

WHAT GOT YOU STARTED IN THE B&B INDUSTRY?

My mother moved with her three children to Vermont in 1978 when I was age 16 and bought the Chipman Inn in Ripton. At the time, the population was fewer than 330 residents. The family had not ever been to Vermont before. But my mother Joan as a child had the dream of running a Vermont country inn after watching the classic movie, White Christmas.

What is your B&B best known for? What is your region known for?

The Chipman Inn is known for providing exceptional and intimate service to our guests. It was built in 1828 by Daniel Chipman, one of three founders of Middlebury College. Ripton is known for being the location of Middlebury College's Summer Mountain Campus called Bread Loaf, a graduate school for English and Literature. It is also known for the Writer's Conference which is held for 11 nights in the summer immediately following the conclusion of the graduate school. Robert Frost lived in Ripton for 39 summers and he is one of the founders of the Writer's Conference. Middlebury College, which is located 8 miles to the west in Middlebury, owns and operates two Ripton ski areas -- the Snow Bowl and the Rikert Nordic Center. The Long Trail runs the entire length of Vermont and runs through Ripton just four miles to the east of the inn.

What's one piece of advice you would offer to someone looking to open their own B&B?

Be prepared to spend long days operating your inn and spending time with guests. Do not buy an inn with the goal of getting rich; do it only if you possess the passion to do so.

With the travel industry so competitive, how are you able to find guests? What is your most successful marketing avenue and why do you think that is?

Word of mouth, newspaper, magazine articles, advertising in Middlebury College Magazine. On-line travel agents ("OTA's") like Expedia and Booking.com made the most significant impact on revenue in the 8 years that I have owned the inn.

FIFTY-ONE

Bay Tree Manor

4201 Seaford Road,
Seaford, Virginia 23696

∽

Mark & Paige Stephens

- "One of the Most Welcoming" B&Bs in Eastern Virginia 2012, 2013 and 2014 by Virginia Living

- Coastal Virginia Magazine's Readers Choice Award in 2018 as Best Local B&B

WHAT GOT YOU STARTED IN THE B&B INDUSTRY?

Loss of a job, need for additional income, experience in hospitality, desirable location

What is your B&B best known for?

Scrumptious large breakfast, Views of the Chesapeake Bay, Kayaking, Pool, Bird watching, Serenity, Luxurious accommodations

What is your region known for?

History - Yorktown, Jamestown and Colonial Williamsburg, Waterfront - York River, Chesapeake Bay

What's one piece of advice you would offer to someone looking to open their own B&B?

You have to be flexible even if you have set times for availability.

What was the hardest part about opening?

Everything doesn't have to be perfect. If you are sincere and hospitable small imperfections don't matter.

With the travel industry so competitive, how are you able to find guests?

Our reviews are the biggest draw.

What is your most successful marketing avenue and why do you think that is?

Being listed with the big players such as Expedia, Trip Advisor, etc. It's hard to get any Google ranking if you aren't listed with them.

FIFTY-TWO

Cedar Grove Inn

3636 Cedar Grove Rd.
Lebanon, TN 37087

∽

Kim Papineau

WHAT GOT YOU STARTED IN THE B&B INDUSTRY?

The enjoyment of meeting new people and looking for something to do for retirement

What is your B&B best known for?

Quiet, country setting, friendship, hospitality and French toast.

What is your region known for?

Rich in heritage, culture and scenic beauty, Middle Tennessee provides genuine Southern hospitality and delivers an unparalleled creative music experience. Rolling hills and fertile valleys dot the land around Nashville, Tennessee's capital, and the Upper Cumberland.

What's one piece of advice you would offer to someone looking to open their own B&B?

It takes dedication and work

What was the hardest part about opening?

Getting the guest to book

With the travel industry so competitive, how are you able to find guests?

We are on every booking site that I can find

What is your most successful marketing avenue and why do you think that is?

Treating my guests like I want to be treated creates repeat visitors and their referrals.

FIFTY-THREE

Walnut Canyon Cabins

503 Deer Rd
Fredericksburg, Texas 78624

∾

Rhonda & Carl Rubadue

WHAT GOT YOU STARTED IN THE B&B INDUSTRY?

Walnut Canyon Cabins is not really a Bed and Breakfast. We are a guest house property. We own and operate a 7 cabin property in the Texas Hill Country about 15 miles outside of Fredericksburg, Texas. Each cabin is equipped with a full kitchen private bathroom and a deck that has a spectacular view!

We got started looking for a turn key operation as a "soft-retirement" adventure. We did not know a guest house property existed until we had purchased it.

What is your B&B best known for? What is your region known for?

We are known for our views, seclusion, proximity to the Texas Wine Country, the free range chickens and the livestock our guests can hand feed with provided treats.

What's one piece of advice you would offer to someone looking to open their own B&B?

Do not bite off more than you can handle, we work every day, but it is a bit less stress than my old profession as an Executive Chef.

What was the hardest part about opening?

Ours was turn key, learning a new business does take a bit of time, however we jumped right into the fire.

With the travel industry so competitive, how are you able to find guests? What is your most successful marketing avenue and why do you think that is?

TripAdvisor and word of mouth. The OnLine Travel Agencies (OTA's) are very necessary to our success. Our reviews are EVERYTHING. We are a destination stay, and reviews are the primary reason our guests find, come, and stay.

FIFTY-FOUR

Inn at Ellis River

17 Harriman Rd
Jackson, New Hampshire 03846

∽

Mary Kendzierski

The Inn has received various awards over the 35 years it has been a B&B.

- In the 6 years since we have been the owners, 3 years in a row, we were voted Best Bed and Breakfast in the Mt. Washington Valley (2017, 2018 and 2019).

- We were awarded as Trip Advisor "Hall of Famers" having achieved 5-star ratings consistently over a span of 5 years.

- We are in the top 10 percent of hotels across the world according to Trip Advisor studies across the industry in 2020.

WHAT GOT YOU STARTED IN THE B&B INDUSTRY?

My husband John and I worked in the corporate world for more than twenty-five years in Massachusetts. Over time the corporate world changed. After taking a hard look at our quality of life, we determined it was no longer what we wanted to do. We needed a change. It took the sudden death of Mary's 43-year-old brother to wake us up to making that change without further delay – life is too short.

What is your B&B best known for? What is your region known for?

Our Inn is best known for our bacon! Seriously, we joke with our guests that they don't care about us – they come back over and over for our "famous" bacon. We are well-known for our ability to and love of treating our guests like family. Our home is their home. Our guests feel comfortable and cared for.

The region in which we live is the Mount Washington Valley which is known for its majestic mountain ranges – many "4,000-footers" are found here. People come to this area to ski (alpine and Nordic). People also come here to hike, many of these folks love the challenge of the 4,000-footers hoping to achieve hiking all 48. They love to check out all the covered bridges and countless rivers and waterfalls (our Inn's 22 guest rooms are all named after some of the falls in New Hampshire). There are countless restaurants from casual to fine dining. Also, people love the tax-free shopping opportunities in this area.

What's one piece of advice you would offer to someone looking to open their own B&B?

Anyone interested in owning a B & B really needs to make absolute sure this is what they want to do. It is not for everyone. It is multi-faceted and innkeepers wear many different hats. Innkeeping is also very physical so one needs to ensure he/she is up to the challenge of long hours. Anyone going into this business must have an "Inn" it to Win it" attitude. It took us about three years to get a strong groove going being so new to it.

What was the hardest part about opening?

Our Inn was already an established B & B. Therefore, we did not have to "open". However, I think the hardest part was hitting the ground running doing something we'd never done before. It was nerve-wracking but no one could tell. We believe we did a nice job transitioning. Hiring the right staff that will stay on with us for the long-haul was a bit challenging as well but we have struck a nice balance and have a great crew.

With the travel industry so competitive, how are you able to find guests? What is your most successful marketing avenue and why do you think that is?

It is true, as they say, "location, location, location". Our B & B is in Jackson, NH about 12 miles south of Mount Washington and about the same distance from North Conway. We are centrally located to several mountains for skiing, hiking, etc. There are countless outdoor activities all around us so people are already coming here all the time – year-round. We have tremendous "drive-by" activity so people see us – we get strong walk-in activity as a result.

We use Constant Contact a lot to engage people and to advise of any new packages we have or specials going on. Constant Contact has been a good tool for us.

We also use Facebook which is okay as a marketing tool, but great for keeping folks engaged. Our marketing dollars are limited so we do not use a lot of marketing avenues.

We have about 60 percent repeat guests. Much of that has to do with our sense of fun and how we treat people. From those guests, we receive lots of referral activity. Word of mouth is the best we believe.

FIFTY-FIVE

Equinox Inn at Biscuit Hill

717 Colleen Dr
Canyon Lake, TX 78133

Darrin and Keith Hammons

What got you started in the B&B industry?

Started by spending time at boy scout campouts, then staying in cabins and talking about what we would do differently.... Then my husband Keith came across a one day class called "So You Want to Be an Innkeeper?".before the Texas State B&B conference. We attended the class and conference, and ended up walking away with a temporary weekend job (with training offered). We innsat a variety of properties the next 4 years and learned so much!

What is your B&B best known for? What is your region known for?

Anticipating our guests' needs and expectations! We're located halfway between Austin and San Antonio in the Texas Hill Country, a great location for day trips to Fredricksberg, New Braunfels, Boerne...Romantic get-away, relax & reconnect....

What's one piece of advice you would offer to someone looking to open their own B&B?

Do your research, join an aspiring innkeeper group that offers shadowing/OJT, join local, state and national organizations to learn more about the industry, marketing etc. Also- use the resources from the local/regional Small Business Development Center for classes on business plans, QuickBooks, marketing...

What was the hardest part about opening?

All the little decisions. Keith jokes he was worried about how to pay for our business, I was worried what would be my first breakfast. We bought an existing business, the owners were older, so had reduced bookings, had not done much marketing in the past several years, (the B&B had been on the market 4 years). So new website, reservation system, partial name change (blending former-Biscuit Hill name with our name Equinox Inn). I admire those who build from scratch or convert!

With the travel industry so competitive, how are you able to find guests? What is your most successful marketing avenue and why do you think that is?

LOCATION! In Texas- the Hill Country, Gulf Coast, Major Tourist Cities ie San Antonio. Absolutely-An active, attractive website. And consistent information across the search engine platforms ie name, address, phone number. Presence on Google Maps. Now we're getting more word of mouth referrals and 5 star reviews.

FIFTY-SIX

The Sedgwick House

7760 Main St
Hunter, NY 12442

∼

Chris & Florentina

WHAT GOT YOU STARTED IN THE B&B INDUSTRY?

My wife wanted to empower me with the experience and freedom of having and running my own business, making my own schedule and having the flexibility of being around our new born son

What is your B&B best known for? What is your region known for?

Our B&B is located in a ski village and it is known for being close to the slopes, great view of the mountain from the front porch, a homy, clean and family & pet friendly place with plenty of breakfast options!

What's one piece of advice you would offer to someone looking to open their own B&B?

Future owners should plan to assemble a "help" team (plumber, handyman, electrical, lawn care) ready to assist in case of unexpected issues and repairs~

What was the hardest part about opening?

Trying to anticipate needs and operational issues that might appear

With the travel industry so competitive, how are you able to find guests? What is your most successful marketing avenue and why do you think that is?

Through good reviews and by building a solid brand and reputation - we build it an website and use OTS as main channels even though we had to pay higher fees to bring clients to our doors.

FIFTY-SEVEN

Hobble Inn

5 Pleasant Street
Stowe, VT 05672

∼

Mary Skelton

- The Loft was written up in the first issue of Bed and Breakfast magazine, because of its unique mission.

- I offer a complementary week's stay to US Veterans and active duty military personnel as a Thank You for their service. They are welcome to sign the entry wall as a permanent record of their stay.

WHAT GOT YOU STARTED IN THE B&B INDUSTRY?

The Inn is in my childhood home, built in 1860 or so. My parents bought it when I was a baby in 1948. I came back to take care of them 8 years ago, and when they died I opened the B&B. Two years later I renovated the former hayloft over the attached carriage barn, into a lovely one bedroom condo.

What is your B&B best known for? What is your region known for?

We are a four season resort town, mainly known for the ski area, Stowe Mountain Resort. I've run Hobble Inn B&B with 2 bedrooms, and The Loft condo with one bedroom for 5 and 3 years respectively.

What's one piece of advice you would offer to someone looking to open their own B&B?

To anyone thinking about hosting guests, PLEASE check with your local authorities about regulations - fire and safety, any licenses and permits that are required. The health and safety of the traveling public depend on it! Hobble Inn and The Loft are proud to be fully licensed, inspected, registered, and insured. I promote that on my website and all OTA platforms.

What is the most rewarding part of the job?

My favorite part is welcoming guests from around the world! I was told I was "famous" in Israel - I had three weekends in a row with guests from Israel. I asked the last one how they found me. He said that they have the equivalent of "Tripadvisor" there, and one prior guest raved about Hobble Inn, and posted pictures of me and the Inn. So I'm "famous" in Israel!

FIFTY-EIGHT

Pheasant Field Bed and Breakfast

150 Hickorytown Road
Carlisle, PA 17015

Kit & Robin
Innkeepers

WHAT GOT YOU STARTED IN THE B&B INDUSTRY?

Our "stock" answer to this question (b/c we get it a lot) is; "four bottles of wine." The real answer is that, as much as possible, during our travels, we would stay at B&B's. As we would leave a B&B we would comment that it might be fun to do that someday, or I wonder if we could that? Fast forward 20 plus years, we settled into a new chapter of our lives working the corporate world. After working the corporate world for about three years in the northern Virginia area we decided that was not working for us. We did some soul searching and rekindled the thought of being innkeepers. So we dove into an extensive research and due diligence period which included attending a weekend long "Aspiring Innkeepers Workshop," attending numerous B&B industry trade shows, and talking to innkeepers. After about two and a half years of research and searching for a B&B, we landing at Pheasant Field Bed and Breakfast in Carlisle PA and we never looked back.

What is your B&B best known for? What is your region known for?

We are known for our "welcome home" feeling. Most of our guests comment on how they feel so much at home when they stay with us. In addition to that comfortable relaxing feel, we are known for our delicious, healthy breakfasts, our soft, comfortable sheets and our clean rooms. Our region is rural and is known for its rich history. Gettysburg National Battlefield is a short drive and there are numerous outdoor activities for all seasons; kayaking, hiking, fishing, skiing, snowboarding and snow-tubing. The historic town of Carlisle is a hidden gem. It has an eclectic collection of restaurant cuisines and a slew of cute boutique shops.

What's one piece of advice you would offer to someone looking to open their own B&B?

We'll offer two pieces of advice …

1. Know yourself – you have to know that you like people and that you will be around them a large portion of your days

2. Do your research and due diligence – make sure it is a good fit for you. Attend an Aspiring Innkeepers' workshop. Go to B&B trade shows and talk to other innkeepers. Doing these things helped us gain a better understanding of our personal, emotional, and financial needs to purchase an

existing B&B and it helped us decide that the innkeeper life style was a good fit for us.

What was the hardest part about opening?

We purchased an existing B&B so we really did not have to "open" per se. We did have a short transition and then we were off and running. The hardest part for our transition was updating the back office to current technologies (accounting software, online reservations system, new website, etc) while establishing ourselves and our personalities with returning guests and gaining new guests.

With the travel industry so competitive, how are you able to find guests? What is your most successful marketing avenue and why do you think that is?

Over the last eight years we have grown our online presence to be very competitive in our market space. We've modernized our website, we are routinely posting on social media (FaceBook, Instagram, YouTube, etc), and we send frequent newsletters to keep our branding current with our guests. In looking at our Google Analytics, our top five online conversion rates are Google organic search, Google My Business, our website, Bing organic search, and mobile FaceBook. Keeping our content fresh and current is why we remain competitive.

FIFTY-NINE

The Owl's Perch

235 Squally
Robbinsville, NC 28771

∼

Alice Lumbard

- The Owl's Perch opened November 2015 and have earned the Airbnb "superhost" badge for 17 straight quarters.

- We joined Booking.com in July 2016 and have consistently earned a rating above 9 out of 10

- We are proud to brag we have many 5 out of 5 star reviews.

WHAT GOT YOU STARTED IN THE B&B INDUSTRY?

We built our little 200 square foot cabin for our own out of town company. We decided to host from the recommendations of neighbors who do cabin rentals.

What is your B&B best known for? What is your region known for?

For those guests that want to experience a "tiny tree-house like" cabin that sleeps 2 with an amazing wild brook trout creek view in the backwoods of northwest North Carolina. Our county is surrounded by 70% national forest offering many hiking trails, waterfalls, two lakes, several brook streams to fish and is two hours from the Smoky National Park. Nearby sites include the Cherohala Skyway, Joyce Kilmer Forest, the famous "Deals Gap" and "Tail of the Dragon", Fontana Dam, and class V rafting on the Cheoah River.

What's one piece of advice you would offer to someone looking to open their own B&B?

If you enjoy being self employed, enjoy sharing your property and home, give it a try; the reward is worth the work!

What was the hardest part about opening?

The time and effort it took to fill out the different platforms of the online sites.

With the travel industry so competitive, how are you able to find guests? What is your most successful marketing avenue and why do you think that is?

We are on the majority of online sites that advertises our little "tiny treehouse like" cabin that sleeps 2. We offer a fair reasonable rate for breakfast and a non refundable no breakfast rate with no minimum night stay except for just a few holidays. Pictures of the prettiest creek you'll ever see in the backwoods, off the beaten path draw guests to our site. We built The Owl's Perch with attention to detail in an eclectic style. We feel all of the above is our niche in the market.

SIXTY

Inn on the River

205 SW Barnard St
Glen Rose, Texas 76043

~

Pamela Streeter

WHAT GOT YOU STARTED IN THE B&B INDUSTRY?

I have been in the hospitality industry my entire career. I made the decision to leave the corporate world behind and yet the only thing I knew how to do was hotels, so it made sense to invest in a B&B.

What is your B&B best known for? What is your region known for?

Our historic building was a Drugless Sanitarium which was a wellness spa in the 1920s-1940s, we continue the tradition of being a place to come relax, get peace & quiet and reconnect with yourself or friends and family. The region we are located is also known for it's history with dinosaurs and our wildlife preservation, so the fact that we sit on a river and are surrounded by nature and history makes us special.

What's one piece of advice you would offer to someone looking to open their own B&B?

Make sure you understand this is a lifestyle and not a job, you have to decide how engaged you want to be with your guests, meaning are you entertaining them or just giving them a place to sleep and a breakfast.

With the travel industry so competitive, how are you able to find guests? What is your most successful marketing avenue and why do you think that is?

Our property has been in business for 36 years, so we have a large number of repeat clients, admitting we have found that being on Facebook, Instagram, Expedia, Bookings.com are usually for finding new customers. The key is making sure you advertise where your customers are - remember you aren't looking to get locals into your business - you need find your unique selling proposition and push the message in your feeder markets.

SIXTY-ONE

Manayunk Chambers Guest House

168 Gay Street
Philadelphia, Pennsylvania 19127

~

Mark F Jerde
Owner

WHAT GOT YOU STARTED IN THE B&B INDUSTRY?

Creativity, Resourcefulness and the good fortune of purchasing a former Parsonage that has been in my husband's family for over 100 years. My entire career has been devoted to the hospitality industry from high school when I began classes at "The Restaurant School" of Philadelphia where I became a certified Chef and Pastry Chef. After 16 years of honing my culinary skills I returned to school to study the hotel industry and shift my career to working the Front desk in some of Philadelphia's Higher End Hotels. From there I found my truest passion of serving guests to make them very happy and comfortable.

What is your B&B best known for? What is your region known for?

First and foremost is offering clean and comfortable accommodations. Proudly, we are ranked #2 of 27 Bed and Breakfasts in the entire City of Philadelphia according to TripAdvisor. What are we known for? The reviews say it all. Our guests rave about our level of service. I do my best to treat every guest personally and according to what their needs are. People are all as different as their needs and for the reasons they are traveling and visiting Philadelphia. I have a knack to pick up on what they are looking for and the type of visit that would satisfy them most. From there,

I will know if they are interested in chatting or if they prefer to be left alone. Whatever the guest may want I will do my best to have it for them. My culinary experience gives me a great understanding of food and the potential dietary restrictions a guest may have. Whether it be a gluten allergy, food likes or dislikes and even the many various levels of vegetarianism I cater to whatever my guests desire. Secondly, the "City of Brotherly Love", Philadelphia has an incredible list of offerings to satisfy everyone's taste. It is no secret that we are the birthplace of democracy in our wonderful country and so rich in history, culture and art. In fact, we are the first city in the US that has been designated a UNESCO "World Heritage City". Manayunk Chambers Guest House is located in the very hip and artsy district of Manayunk, filled with many interesting shops and restaurants.

What's one piece of advice you would offer to someone looking to open their own B&B?

Do your homework first. Know who your guests are and why they are coming to visit your location by what is attracting them to your area.

What was the hardest part about opening?

The hardest obstacle in opening our B&B was getting the zoning approval from the city. Many jurisdictions are not so giving with change and will have you jumping through hoops when it pertains to changing their zoning rules. Hire a competent real estate lawyer to guide you through the process.

With the travel industry so competitive, how are you able to find guests? What is your most successful marketing avenue and why do you think that is?

Building your market and clientele base can be a slow process if you are starting the business on your own starting from scratch. Reach out to area B&B Associations who can help you get started. Build your online presence and your reputation with Google to build your SEO. Your local credibility is also very valuable within the industry and will reflect who you are as an upstanding businessperson and fine neighbor.

SIXTY-TWO

7F Lodge and Events

16611 Royder Rd
College Station, TX 77845

~

Lisa Wantuck

WHAT GOT YOU STARTED IN THE B&B INDUSTRY?

I started as a hired manager for 7F Lodge in 2016. Worked for 1 year and then our family purchased the B&B and Wedding Venue.

What is your B&B best known for?

Unique themed cabins and our Little White Chapel for weddings.

What is your region known for?

Texas A&M Fighting Aggies

What's one piece of advice you would offer to someone looking to open their own B&B?

It a fast paced business with a lot of working parts. You need to be a "Jack of all Trades" AND "Master All of Them" LOL

What was the hardest part about opening?

We did not open the B&B but purchased an existing business. But even that was not easy with all of the hoops that you have to jump through with the city, the state, the comptroller, the insurance, the bank, the alcohol license, etc.

With the travel industry so competitive, how are you able to find guests?

Social Media Marketing

What is your most successful marketing avenue and why do you think that is?

Facebook and Instagram; it's all you need. We don't even do any print ads anymore. My daughter, Ginger manages ALL of our social media and advertising. She is irreplaceable!

SIXTY-THREE

Snowgoose Pond Bed & Breakfast

10460 E Snowgoose Cir
Palmer, AK 99645

Jinks Greenstreet

WHAT GOT YOU STARTED IN THE B&B INDUSTRY?

I'm not sure exactly . . . other than it was just the right thing at the right time. I've always enjoyed hospitality. We live in Alaska and I've always enjoyed when friends & family come up for visits. I love cooking for them and I love finding ways to make people feel comfortable and even pampered. So this just seemed a good fit for me and the timing just worked for us. Our youngest child had just graduated from high school, so we were empty nesters and ready for something new.

What is your B&B best known for?

Comfortable rooms and a good, freshly prepared hot breakfast. Many B&B's nowadays don't actually "cook" breakfast anymore. We do. No cold cereal or canned biscuits. Fresh baked biscuits, scones or muffins daily. And it's something different every day.---What is your region known for? Well, it's Alaska! :-) We're known for epic scenery, hiking, glaciers, world class fishing, and beautiful wildlife like moose & bear.

What's one piece of advice you would offer to someone looking to open their own B&B?

Make sure you like people. I don't think it's something you could do just for money. And ask yourself if you're the type that can be tolerant of all kinds of people. We have guests from all over the world and everyone is different. Even within our own country, there is such diversity of people, personalities & beliefs. Make sure you're someone that's truly up for that. If you're not, I think this could be really hard.

What was the hardest part about opening?

For us, we actually built a large home that would accommodate a Bed & Breakfast, so for us the hardest part was building it from scratch.

With the travel industry so competitive, how are you able to find guests?

Luckily, Alaska is a huge tourist destination, so guests aren't hard to come by. We do have to think about competition within our own area though. We have tried to set ourselves apart with super comfy rooms and a good hot breakfast.

What is your most successful marketing avenue and why do you think that is?

> I get a bulk of my bookings through Expedia (many of the other online booking sites get their info from Expedia, like Hotels.com & Travelocity as well, so I get reservations from all of those) Expedia is just a big go-to for travelers nowadays. I also have a website and get probably a third of my bookings directly through my website. Trip Advisor is a huge help and it links directly to my website.

SIXTY-FOUR

The Parador Inn

939 Western Ave
Pittsburgh, Pennsylvania 15233

∾

Ed Menzer

WHAT GOT YOU STARTED IN THE B&B INDUSTRY?

I worked large & small hotels for almost 30 years, on the F & B side before I got fed up dealing with the corporate BS and opened my first in in S Florida where I was living at the time. It was a large piece of property five minutes to the beach. In 2005 at the height of land speculation some developer was going to tear it down and build 13 townhouses and offered me an obscene amount of money for it. I took the money and ended up moving back to my hometown of Pittsburgh. A huge mansion with 9 guest rooms, an owner's quarters, a ballroom, large garden area and off-street parking.

What is your B&B best known for? What is your region known for?

Pittsburgh is most known for the steel industry although it was just one of many industries pioneered here. Steel is mainly gone and good for us they were along the river fronts. So as they closed much of that space was turned into parklands. Most of my guests come for the sports teams, culture (many museums) and restaurants (Zagat rated Pittsburgh as the best city for restaurants in2015).

What's one piece of advice you would offer to someone looking to open their own B&B?

Marketing is your weakest strength so pump up the iron. I've tried many concepts (most failed), but many succeeded, you get an idea pursue it!

With the pandemic, Expedia has been huge for me and I hate them. But you can acquire new guests and turn them into your own repeat guests.

What was the hardest part about opening?

Being new with no reputation yet, finding customers with no reviews on the travel sites, there's ways around this. And cash flow you can do a lot of things like not buying a case of bath towels from a big distributor and offer in-kind trade (like giving free lodging to travel writers, visiting people for local news organizations).

With the travel industry so competitive, how are you able to find guests? What is your most successful marketing avenue and why do you think that is?

Repeat guests bring new guests. Work your reputation to bring them back again and again. I have probably 60% of my guests have been here before or are a direct referral from a past guests.

SIXTY-FIVE

The Charleston Inn

755 N Main St
Hendersonville, NC 28792

Tommy and Kathy Crowder

WHAT GOT YOU STARTED IN THE B&B INDUSTRY?

A friend of mine bought the Inn for her daughter to run and that did not work out. She knew I was looking to retire from teaching after 22 years, she offered me the job to run the Inn and 3 years later I purchased the Inn from her.

What is your B&B best known for?

Our Southern hospitality and being the oldest Inn in Henderson County.

What is your region known for?

Our beautiful Mountains and great outdoor activities.

What's one piece of advice you would offer to someone looking to open their own B&B?

I would advise them to open a B&B that has no more than 8 to 10 rooms.

What was the hardest part about opening?

Having to live on the property. In North Carolina someone must live on the property.

With the travel industry so competitive, how are you able to find guests?

The booking companies are a big help, a great website, advertising in towns about 2 to 4 hours away, and we have a wonderful tourism that helps with advertising.

What is your most successful marketing avenue and why do you think that is?

The booking companies such as Expedia and Booking.com bring in the most revenue.

SIXTY-SIX

Inn Of The Turquoise Bear

342 E. Buena Vista ST
Santa Fe, NM 87505

∾

Dan Clark
Owner / Innkeeper

- 5 Bucket List Worthy Experiences in New Mexico

- TripAdvisor 2018 Certificate of Excellence & Hall of Fame

WHAT GOT YOU STARTED IN THE B&B INDUSTRY?

I've always liked the idea of being in the hospitality business. It's a noble profession. I've known I wanted to own an inn for over 30 years as my "second career". I have been a member of Innkeeping Associations for 13 years...seven years before I acquired my Inn. I attended conferences and workshops as an aspiring innkeeper. I found attending workshops for "Selling your Inn" very helpful before I sought to acquire my business.

What is your B&B best known for? What is your region known for?

The Inn of the Turquoise Bear B&B in Santa Fe, New Mexico is known for its Iconic Santa Fe property. It's a 200 year old rambling adobe estate that is authentic Santa Fe lodging with towering pine trees, an acre of lush gardens, and mountain views all just a few minutes walk from Santa Fe's historic plaza. It was the home of Witter Bynner (1881-1968), who for almost 50 years was a prominent citizen of Santa Fe, actively participating in the cultural, artistic, and political life of the city. We are now known for our comfortable rooms, friendly service, Iconic Hospitality, and innovative comfort food. Santa Fe and New Mexico is known for its art culture (300 art galleries and the third largest art market in the world) as well as it's famous Opera, shopping, world class cuisine, and the natural beauty of The Land of Enchantment.

What's one piece of advice you would offer to someone looking to open their own B&B?

It's not about the muffins or beautiful gardens. It's about providing hospitality to guests. If you're not ready to meet and engage with ALL guests, where they want to be met with, you're not ready to own and manage an Inn. It's about guest service and hospitality.

What was the hardest part about opening?

I acquired an Inn that had been in operation for 18 years. It was in need of new energy and many updates. I relocated to Santa Fe, New Mexico in order to acquire and run my inn business. Probably the hardest part was being new to the area since one of the chief advantages of staying at a B&B is receiving expert information on the highlights of the area. It was also difficult honoring what prior guests loved about the Inn while updating your services, breakfast, the physical plant and making it your own.

With the travel industry so competitive, how are you able to find guests? What is your most successful marketing avenue and why do you think that is?

Marketing is almost solely online now. Most prospective guests seem to prefer booking online with many booking via mobile. Approximately 85% of our bookings are done online. During the pandemic we did see an increase of guests booking via telephone. The bulk of our marketing expenses are online with pay per click and other searches online.

SIXTY-SEVEN

The Yorkshire Inn

1135 NY-96
Phelps, NY 14532

∼

Kathe Latch
Innkeeper

WHAT GOT YOU STARTED IN THE B&B INDUSTRY?

I stayed in B&Bs all over England and Scotland on my honeymoon, and fell in love with the personal feel of these small inns. It became my dream to one day own one!

What is your B&B best known for? What is your region known for?

I believe my Inn is best known for its comfortable, homey welcome and our delicious breakfasts. Our inn is located in the Finger Lakes region of New York which has lots of wineries, breweries, distilleries and a cheese trail. It is also an area with lots of outdoor activities like hiking, biking, boating, fishing and wildlife.

What's one piece of advice you would offer to someone looking to open their own B&B?

Be prepared for the work! I think sometimes people open B&Bs thinking it will be "easy money", in reality running an Inn is a lot of work when you factor in housekeeping, meal preparation, administrative and promotional tasks, and of course face to face interaction with your guests. It requires patience, good time management and client focus....but it is SO rewarding!!

What was the hardest part about opening?

In our case there was a lot of renovation work to be done on our 200+ year old house. The initial remodel took us 2 1/2 years, after which we opened, but continued renovating and adding rooms and amenities for another several years. Sometimes local or state licensing can present difficult hurdles as well.

With the travel industry so competitive, how are you able to find guests? What is your most successful marketing avenue and why do you think that is?

Our marketing outreach has been focused on online sources all 17 1/2 years we've been open. We have our own website with a built-in booking engine, but have also benefited hugely from our partnership with Expedia which is our portal to reach all the external partners such as hotels.com, TripAdvisor, booking.com and Expedia itself. This online exposure is vital in today's climate. It has attracted a much younger demographic to our Inn in recent years than we saw when we first opened. We have done some print advertising as well, and have joined the Seneca Lake Wine Trail as associate members, and joined a couple of local chambers of commerce. We have also contributed gift certificates to charitable silent auctions, which has increased our visibility with a different audience.

SIXTY-EIGHT

Black Creek Bed and Breakfast

430 N Riverside Rd
Highland, NY 12528

∼

Dan & Brittany

WHAT GOT YOU STARTED IN THE B&B INDUSTRY?

We got in this industry due to the many B&B's I had visited in the past. I am a people person, so it was a perfect fit.

What is your B&B best known for?

Our B&B is known for our exceptional reviews firstly. Secondly, how spotless the premise is kept. Thirdly, how we take care of each and every guest.

What is your region known for?

The region is the Hudson Valley. Where you can can some of the best food on the planet. we are conveniently located about 15 minutes to the Culinary

Institute of America. Hiking, Biking, Kayaking, skiing, are all part of what brings people to the area. Not to mention the 5 colleges within a 25 drive from our B&B.

What's one piece of advice you would offer to someone looking to open their own B&B?

Best advice is, You need to love what you do. Love your guest. Roll up your sleeves this is hard work.

What was the hardest part about opening?

Getting approval from town.

With the travel industry so competitive, how are you able to find guests? What is your most successful marketing avenue and why do you think that is?

Finding guest was a multi-faceted approach. Website, as well as other travel websites. Marketing ourselves as a new approach to the B&B industry.

SIXTY-NINE

The Gibson House Inn

419 S. Main
Kernersville, NC 27284

Darlene Pearson
Owner/Innkeeper

WHAT GOT YOU STARTED IN THE B&B INDUSTRY?

Many years of staying at B&Bs around the country and the world led us to start our own. We knew what we liked about B&Bs and thought we could create a best of all worlds Inn experience. We found the perfect 1837 property to renovate to realize our dream.

What is your B&B best known for?

1837 property next door to the Historic Korner's Folly and across the street from the Moravian Church in the Historic District of Kernersville, NC What is your region known for? Carolina Blue sunny skies, mid-point between the North Carolina Mountains and the North Carolina and South Carolina Grand Strand beaches. The Triad region of North Carolina, of which Kernersville is part, is also known for the High Point Furniture Market

What's one piece of advice you would offer to someone looking to open their own B&B?

You have to be in the B&B business for the love of it and you need to treat guests like family. A true enjoyment of people is required!

What was the hardest part about opening?

Renovating and getting everything just as we wanted it.

With the travel industry so competitive, how are you able to find guests?

Our Web Site, Social Media and multi-channel booking and marketing.

What is your most successful marketing avenue and why do you think that is?

Social media – Facebook, Instagram and Twitter as well as being part of our local Chamber and networking groups make the difference

SEVENTY

The Dominion House Bed & Breakfast

50 Old Dominion Rd
Blooming Grove, NY 10914

∽

Kathy

WHAT GOT YOU STARTED IN THE B&B INDUSTRY?

> We started the B&B after visiting them and realizing our house was perfect and it was a good retirement business.

What is your B&B best known for? What is your region known for?

Hudson River Valley and close to NYC.

What's one piece of advice you would offer to someone looking to open their own B&B?

Think hard about it, it's a lot of work.

What was the hardest part about opening?

Just getting ready, checking on town approvals, insurance, marketing.

With the travel industry so competitive, how are you able to find guests? What is your most successful marketing avenue and why do you think that is?

Internet of course, good website, now as the years go on online travel agencies that do cost you on your bottom line.

SEVENTY-ONE

Letchworth Farm

8983 Oakland Road
Nunda, NY 14517

∼

Richard & Daisy Trayford

- We are an Airbnb Superhost have a 9.6 rating with Booking.com, 5* with Tripadvisor(etc)

- Recognized by New York dept of Tourism as one of the 15 most unique places to stay in NY.

WHAT GOT YOU STARTED IN THE B&B INDUSTRY?

We saw an opportunity as:

a) We are close to the very popular Letchworth State Park and on the Western fringes of the New York Fingers Lakes Region.

b) We have a large Farm/ Farmhouse and recently added two self contained apartments in a spare barn.

c) We are a working horse farm in a remote area and liked the idea of having interesting guests stay with us.

What is your B&B best known for? What is your region known for?

We were recently acknowledged as one of the 15 most interesting places to stay in the whole of NY! (I love NY/Dept Tourism). That's our answer; a unique farm stay experience in a beautiful part of Western New York.

What's one piece of advice you would offer to someone looking to open their own B&B?

Be prepared - you are taking on a 7 day per week job!

What was the hardest part about opening?

We had to make every bedroom in an 1890's farmhouse fully en-suite without ruining the originality of the home.

With the travel industry so competitive, how are you able to find guests? What is your most successful marketing avenue and why do you think that is?

We are in an underserved area (lots of visitors with few accommodation options) plus we offer a unique farm stay experience with Horseback Trail rides, a swimming pond and 88 acres of private space.

SEVENTY-TWO

Inn at Glencairn

3301 Lawrenceville Rd
Princeton, NJ 08540

∼

Lydia Oakes
Chef and Innkeeper

What got you started in the B&B industry?

I had an opportunity to change my career and when I looked at the things I enjoyed most, they were 1) people, 2) food, and 3) travel. Not wanting to be tied down to a mortgage, I pursued B&B innkeeping as it would allow all three of those interests to be maximized. We had owned the house that is now the B&B, and I was looking for a project to do while I was pregnant with my first child. I tell people it was the ultimate in nesting! I had known I was going to "retire" from my career on Wall Street and really needed a gig that would tap my creative side while giving me the flexibility that a new mother needs. I had no history of hospitality, but I did have the business sense and felt as though the area needed accommodations that the Inn could provide. There were many cookie cutter hotels in the area, but none that really allowed guests to step back in time and experience a stay in an historic home from the Revolutionary War era.

What is your B&B best known for? What is your region known for?

The Inn at Glencairn was the only B&B in the Princeton area when it first opened. The Inn is known for its combination of history, comfort, and style. We are often lauded for providing modern amenities in a meticulously renovated Georgian Manor. Princeton is known for its pivotal role in the Revolutionary War. This home was originally built in 1736 and it is said Washington marched past it on his march from Trenton to Princeton. The house was also used as a Hessian hospital. Currently, central New Jersey is known for its farms, gardens, world class restaurant, universities, and shopping.

What's one piece of advice you would offer to someone looking to open their own B&B?

Many guests have asked me that question. I always tell them to find a B&B owner around them and ask if they can work with them as an intern for a few months. That will open their eyes to all that goes on behind the scenes to keep a B&B up and running.

What was the hardest part about opening?

The hardest part about opening our Inn was adhering to the deadline! We were aiming to be open for Princeton University Graduation weekend which is typically late May, and we were literally finishing up construction, painting, and cleaning the night prior to our first check in. Our contractors were telling each other there was NO way we would be open in time, but with some perseverance and a few "all-nighters" we proved them wrong.

With the travel industry so competitive, how are you able to find guests? What is your most successful marketing avenue and why do you think that is?

Our most successful strategy is word of mouth and self promotion. Many people think you need a marketing guru to advertise for you and increase your exposure. We have been featured in The New York Times, Wall Street Journal and Conde Nast Traveler and it was all because I sent a simple email. Currently, about 35% of our business is repeat since we have such a strong following, and those 35% talk to their friends, which brings us a lot of new business via referral.

SEVENTY-THREE

Bed and Breakfast at Oliver Phelps

252 N. Main St.
Canandaigua, NY 14424

∼

Karin Koepcke

WHAT GOT YOU STARTED IN THE B&B INDUSTRY?

Approx. 20 yrs ago I ran a B&B for a couple who were taking a vacation. I remember how much fun I had meeting many delightful and interesting people. During that time an Opera singer stayed with us, and I remember her singing for everyone at breakfast. It was a very magical time. Now I am a meditation, & yoga instructor(since 2006), and recently moved from Maui (where I am a Principal Therapist at a Yoga Retreat Center called Lumeria Maui) to the finger lakes so that I could begin my dream as a B&B owner, and at the same time begin to offer small yoga and meditation retreats at the B&B.The retreats are currently on pause due to covid mandates. Once they are available they will be small private retreats with a max of 5 guests which will lend to a much more personalized offer.

What is your B&B best known for?

I bought my B&B as a turnkey business. It is the first established B&B in Canandaigua(I am the 5th B&B owner), It is a home that is over 200 yrs old, and was owned by the Phelps family (Oliver Phelps and Nat Gorham are the Founders of …having bought the finger lakes area) and it is best known for having easy access to hiking, biking, wine/beer/cider/ trails, lakes, and only a 10 minute walk into our little tourist city of Canandaigua.

What is your region known for?

Including what the B&B is best known for we also have a large concert venue in Canandaigua, known as CMAC. There are established, as well as a growing number of triathlons, marathons, and other races that bring a variety of people from all over the world. We are year round sporting amazing fall colors, skiing, creeks, waterfalls, beaches in the spring/summer, with our wine trails available year round also.

What's one piece of advice you would offer to someone looking to open their own B&B?

Take a class so that you are aware of what you are getting into…It is a really fun and exciting job, and the better prepared you are the more you will be able to enjoy it.

What was the hardest part about opening?

Because I bought turnkey, opening was simple.

With the travel industry so competitive, how are you able to find guests? What is your most successful marketing avenue and why do you think that is?

I like newsletters, plus I have hired a web professional who is excellent at keeping my website up to date, and sending out newsletters as well as blogging. I also use several OTA's..

SEVENTY-FOUR

Black River Inn Bed and Breakfast

704 70th St
South Haven, Michigan 49090

∾

Bob and Judine Kisielewicz
Owners/Operators

WHAT GOT YOU STARTED IN THE B&B INDUSTRY?

My wife and I came to South Haven for years on day trips and vacations from our home in Lansing, Illinois. We enjoyed the beaches, the sunsets, the Kal Haven Trail and the small town feel. We have always loved to entertain and thought that owning a Bed and Breakfast in our favorite place to relax would be just perfect for us. In 2005 we took a huge leap of faith and bought a place that caught our eye with the Black River on one side and the Kal Haven Trail just about on the other. The 1920's farmhouse had gone through some remodels over the years, but we envisioned its potential as an inn with some major remodeling. In July of 2010 we proudly opened our doors as the Black River Inn Bed and Breakfast. I had competed in the sport of bobsledding for many years mostly in Lake Placid, New York and we decided to name our three rooms after famous Winter Olympic sites. Over the years I think we have succeeded in providing our guests with a truly relaxing getaway and making them feel right at home.

What's one piece of advice you would offer to someone looking to open their own B&B?

You have to be outgoing and caring for your guests. We make it a point to try and engage our guests each morning at breakfast. Most people have great stories to tell and the breakfasts in our communal dining area turn into lively conversations with a great deal of laughter. Our topics run the gamut from families to current events. We talk about their plans for the day and where they ate the night before.

With the travel industry so competitive, how are you able to find guests? What is your most successful marketing avenue and why do you think that is?

Many people rely on reviews especially on Trip Advisor and Google to make their selection. Our reviews on there have been fantastic. We also receive reservations through a booking engine on our local Visitors Bureau website which we are not charged for. This past year we have added the ability to make reservations through OTAs like Expedia. This has increased our bookings but their commission fees are quite large. We encourage people to book directly from our website or by calling us to avoid the 15% commission fee that the OTAs charge.

SEVENTY-FIVE

Blue Dragonfly Inn

600 W. 18th St.
Cimarron, NM 87714

∽

Erin Tawney
Owner

WHAT GOT YOU STARTED IN THE B&B INDUSTRY?

I had an epiphany when I was 24 that I wanted to own and run a B&B. I love to cook, but for small intimate groups, not the hustle of a restaurant. So a B&B is perfect for that. It also allows me to express my creativity in cooking, which my guests have thoroughly enjoyed.

What is your B&B best known for? What is your region known for?

Our facility is best known for how quiet it is, how comfortable, and the food. Our guest rooms all have 6'x6' windows that face west towards the mountains, with our nearest neighbor at least 2 acres away. I get compliments all the time on how comfortable the beds are, how clean everything is, and raves about breakfasts. We are 3 miles from the Philmont Scout Ranch, so during the summer with 25,000 scouts rolling through, it is super busy with parents dropping off/picking up their kids, and officials coming through to spend some time at the ranch. We are also close to Angel Fire and Red River, so we'll get folks staying here because they want to be away from the bustle at the ski areas.

What's one piece of advice you would offer to someone looking to open their own B&B?

We try to stay at other B&B's just to see how they operate (we're all different!) and I'll tell you the two most important things are the bed (it must be comfortable!) and the breakfast, which I think goes without saying. The rest you can learn as you go, but if you're not a people person, you might want to reconsider or at least have someone "on staff" who is.

What was the hardest part about opening?

Taking care of and cooking for guests was a new process to learn to get the timing right without intruding too much. Making sure I ask all the right questions up front and getting my schedule together was probably the toughest. We also did a "soft" opening at first so we weren't figuring it out with several people counting on us at once. It worked out perfect!

With the travel industry so competitive, how are you able to find guests? What is your most successful marketing avenue and why do you think that is?

We have our own website (bluedragonflyinn.com) we use Expedia and AirB&B, we are on Philmont's site of "places to stay", the Cimarron Chamber of Commerce, and word of mouth through our friends. Expedia and AirB&B are probably our most successful venues for bookings due to the ease of use and exposure, as well as the fact that most tourists are from outside the state.

SEVENTY-SIX

Mile Hill B&B

2461 Co Rd 21
Valatie, NY 12184

∼

Maret Halinen

WHAT GOT YOU STARTED IN THE B&B INDUSTRY?

Moved Upstate NY and wanted to find something to do. I enjoy people

What is your B&B best known for? What is your region known for?

Hudson Valley beauty and nature art and hiking skiing and organic food and easy access from NYC or Boston or Canada. Mile Hill B and B is located in Kinderhook which is an old Historic Town. I bring European flare I guess being Scandinavian originally. I also have a great POOL.

What's one piece of advice you would offer to someone looking to open their own B&B?

It is hard work, people can be very demanding so you need lots of patience and also need to like serving people.

What was the hardest part about opening?

Getting the word out there. Also get all your licenses in order, insurance etc. Safety.

With the travel industry so competitive, how are you able to find guests? What is your most successful marketing avenue and why do you think that is?

I am still looking for that avenue. Depends location

SEVENTY-SEVEN

Oak Creek Lodge

21575 Brady Rd
Bannister, Michigan 48807

Tracie Hymer

- Michigan Lake Association.
- **We are rated by Expedia 9.9 in guest reviews.**

What got you started in the B&B industry?

We both enjoy cooking and taking care of others.

What is your B&B best known for? What is your region known for?

Wedding, Relaxing/serene. This is not a destination location, usually people come here to get back to nature and off the grid. Canoe, hiking, rail trails, kayaking, golf, etc...

What's one piece of advice you would offer to someone looking to open their own B&B?

Hire good help

What was the hardest part about opening?

We started from scratch, so it was getting everything together that we needed.

With the travel industry so competitive, how are you able to find guests?

Google and good reviews.

What is your most successful marketing avenue and why do you think that is?

Guests themselves, people rely on the reviews of others when making choices.

SEVENTY-EIGHT

Purple Martin Inn and Nature Center

194 East Freidrich Depot
Rogers City, Michigan 49779

Anne M. Kosiara

WHAT IS YOUR B&B BEST KNOWN FOR?

Unique upbeat eclectic décor and our hospitality. What is your region known for? Natural resources and healthy lifestyle. Bicycling, the most public beachfront per capita in Michigan, fresh air, and a small Norman Rockwell city.

What is one piece of advice you would offer to someone looking to open their own B&B?

When you are done planning you are 80% done with the task. Do not buy or open a B&B unless you have done your work.

What was the hardest part about opening?

Reservation system decisions and understanding how to market.

With the travel industry so competitive, how are you able to find guests?

Word of Mouth.

What is your most successful marketing avenue and why do you think that is?

Word of mouth.

SEVENTY-NINE

Moonshadow Bed & Breakfast

10249 Gibson Road
Hammondsport, NY 14840

Jeanette and Steven Harp

- **Moonshadow has rated #1 in Hammondsport every year since 2015 on Trip Advisor.**

- **We have also been featured in Newsweek as a must-stay destination while visiting the Fingerlakes.**

WHAT GOT YOU STARTED IN THE B&B INDUSTRY?

I grew up in an "open door" home. We always had strangers (mostly international exchange students) around our table so having a B&B is a very natural fit for me. I have always loved to cook and entertain. Previously my husband had a catering company/restaurant and I was in the fashion industry.

What is your B&B best known for? What is your region known for?

We pride ourselves on having a very non-traditional feel to our bed and breakfast. You won't find any doilies or teapot collections here. We come from California originally and love the laid-back California vibe, A little bit of shabby-chic and a little bit hippy too. We are located in the heart of the wine country in Upstate New York, surrounded by the Finger lakes. Most guests come for the award winning wines, but we have a ton of history, museums, nature and Antiquing as well. We are also on the Pottery trail.

What's one piece of advice you would offer to someone looking to open their own B&B?

If you can at all help it, Don't wait until you retire… you'll be too tired! While we were looking for our BnB to buy, we always asked why they wanted to sell. #1 answer was they were too tired. (Or they didn't have a partner/help)

What was the hardest part about opening?

We were lucky enough to buy an existing property that had a great reputation. However, I would say for the most part the hardest part is probably getting the word out.

With the travel industry so competitive, how are you able to find guests? What is your most successful marketing avenue and why do you think that is?

We love Trip Advisor. We tried ads in local magazines, Yelp, and other local avenues. We have found 95% of our guests use Trip Advisor to check out reviews.

EIGHTY

Knob Hill Bed & Breakfast

1105 South Dr
Flint, Michigan 48503

~

Diana Phillips

- 2017 Rising Star award from the Flint and Genesee Chamber of Commerce. This award honors a growing business beyond the startup phase, recognizes strengths related to growth, leadership, operations, innovation, and/or special work in the community.

- 2018 Art of Achievement Frontline Ambassador Award from the Flint and Genesee Chamber of Commerce and Genesee Convention and Visitors Bureau. This award recognizes a hospitality worker in a Genesee county hotel who provides outstanding service to guests staying at the establishment.

WHAT GOT YOU STARTED IN THE B&B INDUSTRY?

We have traveled extensively and stayed in many types of lodging. When I met my husband he owned an old country store with cabins that he rented. I guess I married into the hospitality industry. In addition, growing up my father was a small business owner. I think it takes a certain type of person to start a business. I often tell people that neither my husband nor I have the fear (fear of failure) gene.

What is your B&B best known for? What is your region known for?

Our B&B is best known for hospitality and warmth. Flint is known as the birthplace of General Motors.

What's one piece of advice you would offer to someone looking to open their own B&B?

Anyone wanting to open a B&B should join a B&B association; you can learn so much from the members and the association's programs.

What was the hardest part about opening?

Working with the local regulations.

With the travel industry so competitive, how are you able to find guests? What is your most successful marketing avenue and why do you think that is?

> We originally signed up with booking agencies but now most guests find us on the internet or by word of mouth. A great website is essential!

EIGHTY-ONE

The Bentley Inn

694 Main Ave.
Bay Head, NJ 08742

∼

Glenn Kithcart
Innkeeper

WHAT GOT YOU STARTED IN THE B&B INDUSTRY?

Needed to get out of full time real estate sales and get into something still involving contact with lots of people but without the selling pressure (now they come to me instead of me soliciting them).

What is your B&B best known for? What is your region known for?

We are best known for cleanliness and excellent service. The region is the "Jersey Shore" and is known for summer beach fun and fine dining.

What's one piece of advice you would offer to someone looking to open their own B&B?

Open in a location where there is at least 2 seasons. Our area is a single season.

What was the hardest part about opening?

We bought an established b&b but it's reputation was suffering. It was 2001 and the internet was in it's infancy for booking lodging properties so we got an excellent website and free wifi (wasn't even in demand then) and advertised. It worked, it's important to realize that our location was in moderately high demand already, we just had to show people we were fastidiously clean and caring.

With the travel industry so competitive, how are you able to find guests? What is your most successful marketing avenue and why do you think that is?

Unfortunately we rely on OTA's for a growing percentage of our new customers (some repeat customers use them too because they are so easy to use). We have a high rate of return guests, location guests and "word of mouth" guests so we don't advertise other than having a current website and large email database that we have built with permission from our guests. OTA's are good bookings and are good for institutional advertising. We usually capture direct bookings from guests that first stayed here from an OTA booking. Locally our reputation is stellar and folks recommend us to their "overflow guests."

EIGHTY-TWO

Blessings on State Bed & Breakfast

1109 W State St.
Jacksonville, IL 62650

∼

Gwenn Eyer
Innkeeper

WHAT GOT YOU STARTED IN THE B&B INDUSTRY?

I grew up in a very welcoming home. We lived in a small town and when guests visited, they stayed with us instead of the one local motel, and they came from all over the world. When my husband and I honeymooned in Canada 38 years ago, we stayed in bed & breakfasts to offset the price of the upscale hotels (castle/chateau) I wanted to stay in. One B&B was a vintage mansion like ours. Another was a converted garage. I loved both and thought, "That's what I want to do when I grow up!"

What is your B&B best known for?

Hospitality is our hallmark. I am often amazed that some innkeepers don't make that their first priority. I understand that farm-to-fork is a great idea, eco-friendly, etc. but... I'd rather be known for making people feel welcome and building relationships. My dad's family was known for sharing what they had with others, even when they didn't have much. I grew up with family dinners, church potlucks, Sunday dinners at Ted & Ruth's – everyone generously shared what they had. I say that I inherited the Henderson Hospitality gene.

What is your region known for?

We are in the heart of the Midwest, in farm country. Jacksonville and Springfield, our state capitol 30 minutes away are known for history, including Abraham Lincoln. Jacksonville has maybe 10 homes that are linked to the Underground Railroad. My home is one of many vintage mansions in a town with maybe 30 architectural styles. We have a Hallmark downtown area with small locally owned shops (that are praying to survive COVID, just as we are.) Our Eli Bridge Company makes make of the "Ferris" wheels you see, along with Scrambler and other fair rides.

What's one piece of advice you would offer to someone looking to open their own B&B?

Don't do it just because you have a spare room. True innkeeping is a big investment of your time and talent. Since we bought a very small starter home (850 square feet) and started adopting kids very soon (met our first four kids with two years of our marriage), I spent half my life dreaming about being an innkeeper. I planned, saved pictures, read books, took training... it was a big decision that I worked for 25 years to support before we opened.

What was the hardest part about opening?

I was ready, so this really isn't a good question for me. However, my dream finally came true the year I turned 50. We bought our big old house in October and I planned to open the following spring. Sadly, our two-year-old grandson tragically died in December, so it was very hard to focus on the business. My friends provided great support and I'd previously signed up to have an intern from the local college and she did great work completing assignments for me, i.e., research local hotels and B&B's and… recommend what my prices should be, what packages I should offer, etc. I associated with the local and CVB right away and they' Chamber of Commerce re providing tremendous resources today. I also hold membership in the Chamber of Commerce.

With the travel industry so competitive, how are you able to find guests?

My overall quality/service standards bring in the guests I want through normal B&B channels – in a normal world. However, competition from unregulated Airbnb's in my block have hurt me. They don't pay for my insurance, advertising, listing services, etc. and even through they're in a vintage mansion with antiques they had buckets of money coming and undercut my prices by 1/3, at least. They don't really pull my audience, but some my potential guests have been drawn in through Airbnb. (I have a legit B&B listing on Airbnb, but my prices are higher.)

What is your most successful marketing avenue and why do you think that is?

Satisfied guests are my best resource – they post reviews, sometimes; talk to their friends while they attend events in town, often, pre-COVID-19; post on social and talk to their friends after their stay, often. During COVID-19 I've been focusing on social. I'm a dinosaur – I love to write, but I grit my teeth when I think about blogging and writing a newsletter. They pay off, and I'm trying to rewire my mind. Tell me that I love it! I have a good presence on Facebook and am working to build my Instagram following.

EIGHTY-THREE

West Hill House B&B

1496 W Hill Rd
Warren, Vermont 05674

Peter & Susan

- We are a member of Select Registry, Distinguished Inns of North America.

- Peter was presented with the Vermont 2019 Innkeeper of the Year Award by the VT Chamber. This award is designed specifically to recognize individuals who continue to demonstrate excellence in the operation and management of a Vermont bed & breakfast, inn, hotel or resort, and a commitment to the growth of the local community.

- West Hill House B&B was once again awarded the 5 star Certificate of Excellence by Trip Advisor in 2019 for the 9th consecutive year, and the 5 year "Hall of Fame" award for the fourth successive year. - The B&B was awarded the Trip Advisor "Travelers' Choice" Award in 2020 for being among the top 10% of properties globally. At an Awards Ceremony held on April 20th 2009 in the House Chamber of the Vermont State House, Governor Jim Douglas presented a plaque to Peter and Susan, recognizing West Hill House B&B as a Vermont Green Hotel in the Green Mountain State. (One of the earliest to receive this recognition.)

- We have also been designated as a Green Leader at Gold Level by Trip Advisor.

What got you started in the B&B industry?

Susan's lifelong passion for owning a B&B, her love of cooking, and that we both enjoy offering hospitality to guests

What is your B&B best known for?

Excellent hospitality in central Vermont, with lots of activities year round.

What is your region known for?

The outdoors: skiing, hiking, kayaking, golfing, mountain biking, road biking.

What's one piece of advice you would offer to someone looking to open their own B&B?

Be sure you really love the idea of having guests in your home!

What was the hardest part about opening?

Finding good housekeeping help.

With the travel industry so competitive, how are you able to find guests? What is your most successful marketing avenue and why do you think that is?

The bottom line is having an excellent SEO optimized website. Everything else is secondary.

EIGHTY-FOUR

Mansion on The Mile B&B

228 N N East St.
Indianapolis, IN 46204

∽

Tom Gaunt

WHAT GOT YOU STARTED IN THE B&B INDUSTRY?

> We have enjoyed going to B&B for many years and we always knew we wanted to host a B&B of our own if we had the right home. We started collecting items from trips to other countries like Wales & England along with antiques and furnishings we loved and saw in this future home. Great homes are to be shared and we have felt our home of the past 23 years is too wonderful to not share. We realize we are only caretakers in this world and it is to be shared not hoarded.

What is your B&B best known for? What is your region known for?

We are most known for our warm hospitality, lovely historic Victorian home, and great location in the heart of Indianapolis near to all the great athletic venues like the Colts' Lucas Oil Stadium, Pacers' Bankers Life Field House, and the music venues of White River State Park and Old National Centre, formerly known as the Murat, as well as Mass Avenue where many boutique stores and eateries are located as well as the new Bottleworks along with breweries, a winery, and distilleries close by. Indianapolis is the sports capital the NCAA headquarters/museum is located along the canal along with the Indiana State Museum, Eiteljorg Native American Art Museum, Indiana Historic Museum, along with the Botanical Gardens and the amazing Indianapolis Zoo. While Indianapolis is well known for the largest one day event in the world, the Indianapolis 500 Speedway Race just 2 miles away from our downtown location, our city is known for having more war memorials than any other city outside of Washington, D.C. since it hosts the headquarters for the American Legion for nearly 100 years.

What's one piece of advice you would offer to someone looking to open their own B&B?

To be a successful B&B one must be patient, flexible, enjoy people, be comfortable with others in your home, choose the right location for your targeted cliental, have an interesting property, and have the ability to do much of the work and cost yourselves.

What was the hardest part about opening?

The hardest thing about opening is greeting the very first guest to your B&B. We practiced on friends and gave free rooms to deserving people who had children in the hospital. They appreciated it and helped us critique our service and accommodations from an outsiders view. This helped realize our weaknesses or adjustments we needed to make.

With the travel industry so competitive, how are you able to find guests? What is your most successful marketing avenue and why do you think that is?

We have relied much on word of mouth and excellent reviews from day one. When we first opened we had a guest from Shanghai, China who greeted us stating he heard we had excellent cookies. Up until that time we had used no form of advertising or booking arrangements outside of ourselves. The Chinese gentleman had heard of our B&B thru a previous guest. Needless to say, word of mouth half way around the world lets you know, you have a good reputation. Our guests continue to tell us, they chose us because of our excellent reviews posted on Booking.com (9.8) and Expedia (10) as well as awards for the Best Hotel in Indianapolis for 2019 & 2020. Our guests enjoy a beautiful full breakfast served on English china in a formal Victorian dining room accompanied with music played by the hostess from a grand piano in the parlor.

EIGHTY-FIVE

The Blue Horse Inn

3 Church Street
Woodstock, VT 05091

∼

Jill Amato

WHAT GOT YOU STARTED IN THE B&B INDUSTRY?

With careers in human resources and education in a major metropolitan area, we decided to use our people skills, and creativity to work in hospitality in our favorite state (Vermont). The search for the perfect property took on a life of its own. Six years later, we purchased a fixer-upper in a picture-perfect New England town.

What is your B&B best known for?

Here is a quote from a recent TripAdvisor review: "The best word I can use to describe the Blue Horse Inn is idyllic. From the Colonial brick facade to the sprawling and well-manicured grounds and seasonal decorations you might think you stepped onto the backlot of a studio filming a show like Gilmore Girls. The Blue Horse in is beautiful; It's warm, cozy, comfortable and every other curled up by the fireplace with a warm cup of coffee adjective you can think of." The Blue Horse Inn was built in 1831, yet it has been updated to appeal to folks of all ages. This is not an inn filled with doilies and knick-knacks! We offer modern conveniences along with the charm of a grand, antique home.

What is your region known for?

Picture this: babbling rivers, covered bridges, cows in pastures, red barns, and rolling hills. Nestled in this ideal nature, a quintessential New England town with historic mansions adorning a Green. The village will enchant you with its quaint stores, art galleries, cafes and restaurants. Summertime offers farm markets, festivals, and concerts, as well as hiking, biking, rafting and horse back riding. Our fall foliage will wow you, and our nearby ski slopes will entertain you in the winter.

What's one piece of advice you would offer to someone looking to open their own B&B?

Take your time to find the right property. Don't be too idealistic. It is easy to fall in love with a charming property that may not make good sense from a business perspective. Location is the most important aspect of choosing the right property.

What was the hardest part about opening?

Since we were a start-up with no experience in hospitality, it took time for us to work out the flow of daily operations. My (art) teacher skills were key in learning to plan and prep for success to run the breakfast service at our inn, and my husband's enchanting people skills and keen business sense helped balance our skill set to work effectively together as a team.

With the travel industry so competitive, how are you able to find guests? What is your most successful marketing avenue and why do you think that is?

Being in a destination location was key to getting our business started. Our first bookings were from guests looking for rooms to attend local weddings before we even began to advertise for business. After that, guest reviews and a strong website with quality photos really helped our business grow. We have only done a little print advertising (magazines, etc.), and we are active on social media. Based on my conversations with guests, reviews and word of mouth advertising are key to our success, possibly because our town is a destination for regional travelers.

EIGHTY-SIX

Oft's Bed and Breakfast

11523 N 156th St.
Bennington, Nebraska 68007

∼

Gordon and Linda Mueller

- Property is listed on the: "National Register of Historic Places".

- "Hidden Treasure Award" from the Nebraska Heritage Program

- Recently featured in: "Luxurious Living Magazine"

- Featured in: "Only in Nebraska".

- Identified as one of the "Romantic Places to Stay" in Nebraska.

WHAT GOT YOU STARTED IN THE B&B INDUSTRY?

My mother passed away leaving the family home to us, making me the fourth generation to live in the home my great grandparents built.

What is your B&B best known for?

Our warm hospitality, food and cleanliness.

What is your region known for?

The Midwest is known for its corn fields, farms and friendly people.

What's one piece of advice you would offer to someone looking to open their own B&B?

It's critical you have to enjoy being around people.

What was the hardest part about opening?

Waiting for the phone to ring.

With the travel industry so competitive, how are you able to find guests?

The internet is essential.

What is your most successful marketing avenue and why do you think that is?

Marketing avenues continue to change due to technology and changes in social trends. Marketing is a moving target.

EIGHTY-SEVEN

Cucharas River Bed and Breakfast

90 Cuchara Ave
La Veta, Colorado 81055

Gaylene Smith

WHAT GOT YOU STARTED IN THE B&B INDUSTRY?

> I have always enjoyed hosting. I got an opportunity to purchase this great house in Cuchara, CO in 2018. My first time staying at a B&B was back in 1996 in New Hampshire. I knew then that I would truly enjoy owning my own.

What is your B&B best known for?

> Being a Home Away From Home, my hospitality, breakfast, location, and a great host dog Riley.

What is your region known for?

> Fishing, Hiking, Hunting and beautiful location in the southern part of Colorado.

What's one piece of advice you would offer to someone looking to open their own B&B?

> Be prepared to work 24 - 7 365 days of the year. Also try not to do it all yourself.

What was the hardest part about opening?

> For me it was situations that were out of my control. I purchased in May 2018 and opened June 2018. Then we had a forest fire occur on June 26th and had to evacuated for 10 days which ended up over the busiest time of the year (July 4th week).

With the travel industry so competitive, how are you able to find guests?

Word of mouth has been one of my best ways. I also market through Expedia and AirBnB. I have my own website also cucharasriverband-b.com and Facebook.

What is your most successful marketing avenue and why do you think that is?

Word of Mouth. Once you have stayed at my B&B you always want to come back.

EIGHTY-EIGHT

Birchwood Inn

7 Hubbard St.
Lenox, MA 01240

∼

Tom Johnson and Debbie Lancaster
Innkeeper/Owners

WHAT GOT YOU STARTED IN THE B&B INDUSTRY?

Driving 45 minutes into the city of St. Louis everyday for work and then an hour or an hour and a half, depending on traffic to get home, I asked Debbie if this was what she wanted to do for the next ten years. She loves to cook and her brother in England had used one bedroom of his house as a B&B, which he thoroughly enjoyed. So after some discussion about where we might locate to be the most successful, we thought we would go to Maine. After a trip there we discovered that might not be the best place for a year round business. We completed a weekend long course on how to run a B&B and how to buy a B&B. After the course the instructor met with us and gave us a list of eight or ten places to go see. All were good businesses and the owners were retiring, sick, or done being innkeepers. After a long road trip to see all of the inns, and comparing all the benefits of each site, we chose this one.

What is your B&B best known for? What is your region known for?

The Birchwood Inn has been an inn since 1971 and has always prided itself on its hospitality and good cooking. Because we are located in the western part of Massachusetts known as the Berkshires, we are known as the summer home of the Boston Symphony Orchestra and the Tanglewood outdoor music venue that hosts them and other concerts including artists as varied as Diana Ross, Steve Martin, Josh Groban, Sting and Train. Besides Tanglewood, the Berkshires boasts five live playhouse theaters and includes Jacob's Pillow, the indoor/outdoor theater that is dedicated to dance. In the early 1900s the Berkshires was the summer home of the ultra-wealthy such as the Vanderbilts, Rockefellers and Morgans, and to this day has several of their properties open to the public for tours. The fall is all about "leaf peeping" and the winter is for hiking, skiing, snowshoeing and curling up by the fireside with a good story. Lenox is twenty minutes south from Mount Greylock, the tallest mountain in Massachusetts and twenty minutes north from Bash Bish Falls, the tallest waterfall in Massachusetts.

What's one piece of advice you would offer to someone looking to open their own B&B?

Greet the guests, be available and be friendly. Remember, your guests are typically on vacation and want to enjoy themselves. It is all about the guest experience.

What was the hardest part about opening?

We had closing on a Tuesday in June and were open the next day, just before the busy season started. Had we not had the previous assistant innkeeper agree to stay on while we adjusted, we would have been floundering with learning how to deal with housekeeping, cooking, reservations, permitting and inspections.

With the travel industry so competitive, how are you able to find guests? What is your most successful marketing avenue and why do you think that is?

If we could succeed without the online travel agencies, OTAs, we would drop them and never look back; however, because they dominate search results on the web and dedicate teams of people to reach the top of the list, we have come to discover that the big three or four OTAs capture almost fifty percent of our bookings. We have also discovered that the hospitality we offer has moved us up in reviews created by guests, which also brings new guests.

Our one most successful marketing avenue is being located in a town known for tourism. During the busy season, we could rent twice as many rooms as we have. We added a gazebo on the property and advertise on our web page for small weddings and elopements as well as with wedding planners.

EIGHTY-NINE

Nola's Onekama Hideout

8195 5th St.
Onekama, Michigan 49675

∼

Nola Teye
Owner/Operator

WHAT GOT YOU STARTED IN THE B&B INDUSTRY?

First Brief History:

I worked in corporate America for most my life, then something changed during the dumbing down of America, they no longer valued the workers with knowledge and good work ethics. They were hiring workers who did nothing but play on their phones, and did FB on their computers. Paid them more and left the rest of us to do all the work for less pay. That did not sit well with myself, so I started thinking "a lot"

I have a big love for people and my gifts are service, so I started by helping 3 beautiful ladies with light housekeeping, small maintenance, when I realized they were lonely, very lonely. We became the best of friends and I loved them all very much in their own special uniqueness.

This was not enough income to meet my expenses, so I decided to pack it up and move back to Michigan where my grandchildren were and my aging parents. So I ended up in Newaygo, Mi then when walking one day I saw a sign for innkeeper at the local B&B, and I remembered the words of one of these dear women I helped. Nola you would make a wonderful Bed & Breakfast owner. I knew nothing of what it would take, so I applied and got the position. I wouldn't have to find a place of my own, I would live on the property and run it.

I woke every morning at 5:30 and made breakfast for 6 to 20 persons each morning, at first it was a buffet breakfast as they had always done, they i found more and more had health issues, vegan, whatever the issue or desire, I started making single plates for each quest with whatever they wished for breakfast. A little hairy at times, but always given grace for my efforts. People who come to Bed & Breakfast are different from the ones who go to Hotels, Motels. They want interaction, some are lonely, some curious, some just enjoy life and people and want to know all about you.

I would serve anything from Crepes, Pancakes, Eggs (any way), bacon, sausage, yogurt, oatmeal, Hash Browns, and fresh bakery made myself.

I maintained the lawn, flower beds, snow shoveling, snowblowing, cleaning, bedding, dishes, cooking. They were long days, but oh I learned so much and knew I loved this lifestyle enough to purchase my own.

I worked at Newaygo B&B for one year to the day, they moved to Onekama, Mi to run my own and be near my parents. What I learned from here is just be yourself, be genuine.

I looked one day and found my property, it took months to buy because the Village here does not allow bed and breakfasts here in the village. So I found a common friend here to help me and I found a way around. I am called a Vacation Rental, ran as closely as a Bed & Breakfast as possible.

I do most of the work here, lawn, maintenance, cleaning, booking, greeting, etc. "all of it" except for plowing drives, and some mechanically I can't figure out. I work most days from 6 am till 10-11pm. I love every second when busy with family and friends.

What is your B&B best known for?

Best knows for Nola (I have a personality that draws people or chases them away) Most return here because I treat everyone like family. "Word of Mouth my best Advertising"

What is your region known for?

Lake Michigan, Hiking Trails, Skiing, SnowMobiling (but Onekama won't allow trails thru their Village) Sleepy Bear Sand Dunes, Leelanau Peninsula (wine country)

What's one piece of advice you would offer to someone looking to open their own B&B?

Don't be afraid of Hard Work and Long Days they will pay off. I do this alone, and it is hard for a couple to compliment each other and take on responsibilities.

What was the hardest part about opening?

The Village RoadBlocks - Building up supplies, furnishing it. I did a go fund me page, I was given quite a bit of items I could use, The second year I spent a lot of the money made on better, comforters, sheets, towels, and a few pieces of furniture, working on lawn equipment this next year, and a part time person to help clean rooms. One step at a time.

With the travel industry so competitive, how are you able to find guests?

(Word of Mouth) When guests leave happy and feeling loved they come back, they tell their friends.

What is your most successful marketing avenue and why do you think that is?

Google, AirBnB, Booking.com - Google everyone uses now a days, they can call you right from the look up, AirBnB is everywhere all over the world, they do a very good job, my favorite to host guests from AirBnB, Booking.com a certain group of persons use this booking agent and they are good guests.

NINETY

Ashley Manor

3660 Main Street
Barnstable, MA 02630

∽

Keith and Allison McDonald
Proprietors

- Trip Advisors Travelers Choice Award for 2020. Top 10% of Hotels worldwide

- AAA Best of Housekeeping for 2020

WHAT GOT YOU STARTED IN THE B&B INDUSTRY?

My wife Allison and I got started in the business due to our extensive backgrounds in the Hotel, Restaurant and Culinary Industries.

What is your B&B best known for? What is your region known for?

Our B&B is best known for our hospitality. Our region is best known for its beaches (Cape Cod)

What's one piece of advice you would offer to someone looking to open their own B&B?

There isn't one piece of advice because the industry isn't one size fits all. But I would say follow your heart! Not all industry leaders are right with their advice when it comes to selecting a business. Also new owners should make sure they are inheriting a stellar reputation.

What was the hardest part about opening?

The hardest part for us aside from being hit with a pandemic was leaving our families in California.

With the travel industry so competitive, how are you able to find guests? What is your most successful marketing avenue and why do you think that is?

Finding guests comes down to the reputation I mentioned. Building a new client base through word of mouth and positive reviews are priceless.

NINETY-ONE

Irving House at Harvard

24 Irving Street
Cambridge, MA 02138

Rachael Solem
Owner and General Manager

**IRVING
HOUSe**
at HARVARD

- Board Member, Cambridge Local First

- Board Member, Harvard Square Business Association
- Board Member, Massachusetts Lodging Association
- President, Cambridge Hotel Association

What got you started in the B&B industry?

My partners and I saw a sad-looking house on a lovely street in a great location. It happened to be an operating guesthouse.

What is your B&B best known for?

Irving House has been hosting Harvard University affiliates since the 1920s. We are known for our convenience and friendliness.

What is your region known for?

Universities, history and culture

What's one piece of advice you would offer to someone looking to open their own B&B?

Location matters a great deal. Know your market!

What was the hardest part about opening?

Doing all the repairs and improvements while still accommodating guests. Glad that's over!

With the travel industry so competitive, how are you able to find guests?

We are now relying on our returning guests, sending out a newsletter with more than 5,000 subscribers. Many cannot travel just now, but let us know they are still thinking of us.

What is your most successful marketing avenue and why do you think that is?

We market to Harvard offices, and other university offices, making it easy for them to book with us.

NINETY-TWO

The Wayward Traveler's Inn

2398 N. Singleton Avenue
Mims, FL 32754

∽

Tina Adamson

- For the years 2019 and 2020 we have received a 9.6 rating (out of 10.0) from Hotels.com for "Most Wanted Award". This is based on overall customer ratings.

WHAT GOT YOU STARTED IN THE B&B INDUSTRY?

It was a fluke.... I needed a large home because I thought I had a daughter and grandchildren moving in. We all moved in and after just 3 months she moved out so we looked at ourselves and said, "I guess we're going to run a Bed & Breakfast!"

What is your B&B best known for? What is your region known for?

We are a very comfortable homey style atmosphere with old southern charm. We are in a small town in Brevard Co Florida, close to Kennedy Space Center, lagoons where you can see bioluminescence, dolphins and manatees.

What's one piece of advice you would offer to someone looking to open their own B&B?

Get as many local connections with other businesses and the Chamber of Commerce as possible.

What was the hardest part about opening?

Actually it was easy because the sellers allowed us to "purchase"all of the proprietary information, name, website, etc., so there was already a presence of the inn being run under this name.

With the travel industry so competitive, how are you able to find guests? What is your most successful marketing avenue and why do you think that is?

We got an account with Expedia and come up in searches in this area with all other hotels. We got professional pictures to help with our image.

NINETY-THREE

Main Street Bed & Breakfast

208 E Main St
Glasgow, KY 42141

~

Cherie Vaughan
Owner/Innkeeper

WHAT GOT YOU STARTED IN THE B&B INDUSTRY?

> My friend asked me to take over one of her B&Bs.

What is your B&B best known for? What is your region known for?

> My delicious breakfasts, and Mammoth Cave

What's one piece of advice you would offer to someone looking to open their own B&B?

It is important your location has a draw to bring people there. A reason to come.

What was the hardest part about opening?

Getting the word out.

With the travel industry so competitive, how are you able to find guests? What is your most successful marketing avenue and why do you think that is?

Word of mouth through Social Media. More of my business is now coming directly rather than through the OTAs.

NINETY-FOUR

Beall Mansion An Elegant Bed & Breakfast Inn

407 E. 12th St.
Alton, IL 62002

∼

Jim & Sandy Belote

- "National Geographic Map Guide Destination"

- "TripAdvisor Hall of Fame" Award Winning Property

- "50 Best B&Bs in America" -The Daily Meal

-" USA Top 100 Gold Inn & B&B" Award Winning Property

- "Top 30 Bed and Breakfast" -Midwest Living

-" Best Illinois Bed & Breakfast" -Illinois Magazine Readers Poll

- "Top 25 Romantic Getaway" -BBW Magazine

- "Top 3% of accommodations worldwide for customer satisfaction" - HotelsCombined

WHAT GOT YOU STARTED IN THE B&B INDUSTRY?

(a) We were looking for a home that could accommodate aging parents and got carried away.

(b) My wife, Sandy, always enjoyed people, entertaining, and providing hospitality. What better fit than a bed & breakfast?

What is your B&B best known for?

Award winning accommodations for leisure, bleisure, and business, and in non COVID times, our 24 hour all you can eat chocolate, chocolate, chocolate buffet.

What is your region known for?

There is only 1 place in America where 2 of the nation's great roadways (Route 66 and the Great River Road) come together alongside the confluence of America's 3 great rivers (the Mississippi, Missouri, and Illinois River)—the Great Rivers & Routes region. There is only 1 Gateway to the West—the St. Louis area. The BEALL MANSION is proud to be part of both. For a complete lists of things to do please visit: riversandroutes.com and explorestlouis.com

What's one piece of advice you would offer to someone looking to open their own B&B?

Find a bed & breakfast similar to the type you would like to own. For example, is you dream bed & breakfast upscale, rustic, urban, country, couples only, family oriented, pet friendly, etc. Once you have done so, talk with the innkeepers about booking a week or 2 at their property in exchange for the opportunity to pick their brain and get real-world hands on experience. By the end of your stay you should have a really good idea whether innkeeping and owning that type of inn is a good fit for you.

What was the hardest part about opening?

In our case, we purchased a historic home and had it restored and converted for use as a bed & breakfast. Dealing with licenses, contractors, delays, unforeseen problems, etc. was by far the most challenging. Although purchasing an operating bed and breakfast that somebody else has restored and converted will cost more up front, chances are that in the long run it will save you loads of money, time, and perhaps even your sanity.

With the travel industry so competitive, how are you able to find guests? What is your most successful marketing avenue and why do you think that is?

Having a unique property, good relationship with the area convention & visitors bureau, and a search engine friendly website are key.

NINETY-FIVE

Serenity Hill Bed and Breakfast

3600 MAMMOTH CAVE ROAD,
BROWNSVILLE, KY

∼

Tina Burr

FROM THE OWNER:

I am Tina Burr, the owner of Serenity Hill Bed and Breakfast in Brownsville, KY. I got my start in the B&B industry was a fluke. My husband and I talked about owning our own B&B one day, but time just never seemed right. One day my husband and I were talking when we decided we wanted a bigger house, so we went looking and found this home we liked. We called a realtor and gave her what we were looking for. One day she called and told us about a house for sale that we might like. We scheduled a viewing. As soon as I drove up the driveway, I fell in love with the view, and everything I was looking at. We walked up to porch and entered the house. I was blown away again by what I was shown. I was in love with the house and imagined us living there. While speaking with the owner we found out we were at a fully open and running B&B. I told my husband I wanted house. He said we can close the bed and breakfast and live in it as a home. I said let's try running the business. My husband said he couldn't help because he already had a job. I said I will do it and if I couldn't do it or liked running it we could close it up. I have never been or even ran a business before. I was nervous about doing so. I was so nervous and scared at the same time upon meeting and greeting my first ever guests, not knowing anything about what I was doing or supposed to do, but I decided to just be myself and sink or swim on my own. I ran with how I wanted to run my business and have loved every moment of what I do. I treat everyone the way I want to be treated. Now after two years, I still love what I do and all the people I have met along the way. Everyone who stays here is now family or forever friends. I thank God everyday for my wonderful life. I am a very lucky person to also have such a loving and supportive husband. I have the best of two worlds. There isn't a day that I don't have a smile on my face because I love what I do. Guests are more relaxed when they see how much you enjoy what you do. This is not a job to me at all. This is my passion. Serenity Hill Bed and Breakfast is know for its location to Mammoth Cave National Park in Cave City, KY. Serenity Hill Bed and Breakfast is one mile from cave, many trails, as well as many other things to do and places to see We try and give suggestions on things to do while in the area as well as to suggestions on local places to eat. All my guests either find us via referrals, online searches, or on website of ours. We use previous guest referrals, advertise through Mammoth Cave, national corvette site, resnexus, booking, convention centers, just to name a few. I honestly believe my bed and breakfast speaks for itself by all the wonderful reviews it receives, as well as all my guest referrals. The most rewarding part of running my bed and breakfast is all the people I get to interact with. I start my day by getting up at 6am every morning and by 6:30am all breakfast beverages are set out. A huge country breakfast is served at 8am. After breakfast we clean and sanitize rooms to get ready for next guests. Then I have rest of day to do what I need to do, whether that be paying bills, laundry, etc. Being a good cook or having a good cook will be a plus in this line of work. Always remember to love what you do and all your hard work will pay off tremendously. One person can run a 5 room or less B&B if they want to but not if they don't have the love or passion to do it. If you have a bigger B&B, you are definitely going to need help. If you are busy with current guests and have more check-ins immediately following as well as check-outs all at same time can be a little hectic at times but if you stay true to yourself and stay patient, all will work out. Sites like Airbnb have very little impact on B&B's. I have been known to get some Airbnb guests stay with us from time to time. We all work with one another to make each other successful. It's not a competition, because there is plenty of room for everyone.

We have awards for being a porch partner with a mothers rest, certificate of excellence from corvettes as well as trip advisor, a 10 rating certificate from booking.com, just to nam a few our reviews and guest referrals are our best marketing avenue. Serenity Hill Bed and Breakfast is open year round from 24 hours a day. I will text you shortly with recipe and pics, as well as pic of house and logo. Thank you for allowing us the opportunity to be in your book. Good luck and can't wait to read your book

---

NINETY-SIX

Sylvan Falls Mill B&B

156 Taylors Chapel Rd
Rabun Gap, GA 30568

∽

Linda Johnson

Certified Green establishment 2015 to present

WHAT GOT YOU STARTED IN THE B&B INDUSTRY?

Working in the service industry in college

What is your B&B best known for? What is your region known for?

Comfort and good food...great outdoor activities

What's one piece of advice you would offer to someone looking to open their own B&B?

Do as much research as possible including hands on working and if working with spouse, make sure you are compatible business associates.

What was the hardest part about opening?

Thinking you are ready... best to set a date and then stick to it... everything is never perfect

With the travel industry so competitive, how are you able to find guests? What is your most successful marketing avenue and why do you think that is?

Internet website and word of mouth.

NINETY-SEVEN

Kilgore Mountain Hideaway B&B

3302 Lariat Rd
Island Park, Idaho 83429

What got you started in the B&B industry?

I had turned my home into a hostel to fund my humanitarian work. I live near Grand Teton National Park and am 2 hours from Yellowstone National Park. Guests were driving the two hours to Yellowstone because it is so expensive to stay in West Yellowstone so I knew I could do well if I was closer to Yellowstone. I found this beautiful lodge and cabin for sell just 45 minutes from the west entrance of Yellowstone and turned it into a bed and breakfast. (We do a continental breakfast only so do not cook anything. Guests can also cook dinner there too.)

What is your B&B best known for? What is your region known for?

It's best known for its remote setting, with wildflowers and wild animals in abundance. It is near Yellowstone National Park and the area has great hiking, fishing and other outdoor activities. In the winter I rent out the whole lodge to groups of snowmobilers as it is one of the best places in the United States to snowmobile!

What's one piece of advice you would offer to someone looking to open their own B&B?

Make sure you are in an area that people like to travel to.

What was the hardest part about opening?

Finding good help!!!

With the travel industry so competitive, how are you able to find guests? What is your most successful marketing avenue and why do you think that is?

I am listed on all the major booking sites: booking.com (which also owns Priceline), Expedia.com (which owns MANY other booking sites like hotels.com, Trivago, Homeaway), Hostelworld, Airbnb and I have my own website which if guests can find has the best prices! So being listed on all those sites that are used my 99.9% of guests makes me easily found. I also make sure my prices are very competitive.

NINETY-EIGHT

Surf Song Bed & Breakfast

21 Officers Row
Tybee Island GA 31328

~

Jeremy

WHAT GOT YOU STARTED IN THE B&B INDUSTRY?

It's been my wife's life-long dream to own a bed and breakfast. Her teaching career wasn't headed where we expected - and was not fulfilling. We decided to take the plunge and move to warmer weather while we were at it.

What is your B&B best known for? What is your region known for?

We are located on Tybee Island, just outside of Savannah, GA. Our inn is 300 steps from the Atlantic ocean, where we have private beach access. We get high marks for friendly service and clean rooms. Tybee Island is one of the barrier islands off the coast of Georgia. You're forgiven if you were not aware there are islands in GA. Having come from Michigan, most of our friends and family had never heard of it. Tybee has been called the "Redneck Riviera" - but in a nice way. That means it's a laid-back atmosphere set in a stunningly beautiful locale.

What's one piece of advice you would offer to someone looking to open their own B&B

Oof, where to start? How 'bout don't do nine months before the start of a global pandemic? I guess, one thing that we figured out is that you really should look to buy an existing business. It just removes so many unknowns from the equation, there's no downtime, a built in customer base, and most importantly, the bank will likely only lend on an existing business.

What was the hardest part about opening?

Well, since we took over an existing business, there wasn't really a grand opening. We didn't change the name, or even the curtains for that matter. However, there were other struggles. We took over in the middle of the busy season. We had to juggle the move, financing, finding a school for the boys, etc...all while running the business.

With the travel industry so competitive, how are you able to find guests? What is your most successful marketing avenue and why do you think that is?

We chose a good location. Tybee is a vacation destination, so the people will come. That said, we do have to fight against hotels, other B&Bs, and AirBnb. In my opinion, the best marketing you can do is to have a high rating on google and have the lowest price among your peers. It's imperative to have an excellent website. Other that that, I'm not convinced traditional marketing works.

NINETY-NINE

Hilo Bay Hale Bed and Breakfast

301 Ponahawai St, Hilo, HI 96720

~

Matthew Potts
Owner

What got you started in the B&B industry?

I got started in the B&B business in 2008 during the "economic downturn". When everyone around me was losing their career or job to the crash. I asked myself "what do you want to do?...not what do you have to do". The answer was move home to Hawaii and save a 1912 plantation home from demolition and remodel it to become a B&B.

What is your B&B best known for? What is your region known for?

The Hilo Bay Hale is best known for providing a comfortable clean place to stay with an outstanding breakfast with items like coffee eggs Papaya bananas and pineapples all grown on our farm in Pahoa. Our reviews reflect our aloha spirit as our strongest quality. Our area is most known for volcanoes national park and the beauty of the land and water that is Hawai'i nei.

What's one piece of advice you would offer to someone looking to open their own B&B?

Give yourself another place to stay. I have the farm 30 minutes away. Thus way I don't burn out. I'm not living at my job. Give yourself two days consecutive off per week. Be kind to all people. Live aloha

What was the hardest part about opening?

18 month remodel. Apply for permits early.

With the travel industry so competitive, how are you able to find guests? What is your most successful marketing avenue and why do you think that is?

We are competitive but supportive in our community. We use word of mouth and can successfully recommend places based on what each guest bay gets looking for. Well directed recommendations and knowing who among your competition may make a good recommendation is key. Internet. Find as much free advertising as you can. Reviews are so important. It's what drives your reservations.

ONE HUNDRED

Avalon Bed & Breakfast

1317 Duval Street,
Key West, FL 33040

∽

Yvonne

WHAT GOT YOU STARTED IN THE B&B INDUSTRY?

I was working as a health inspector for Div of Hotels and Restaurants. I missed the hotel industry and you can really only stab raw chicken so many times with a thermometer before looking for something else. No one is ever happy to see the health inspector. I was inspecting the B & B when I mentioned this and was offered the job.

What is your B&B best known for? What is your region known for?

B & B - Christmas Lights (We go to town at Christmas, takes me 12 hours to decorate the front of the house), Romantic ambiance, Excellent location (Duval Street), cleanliness. Key West - Is Key West what else is there to say. One Human Family, Southernmost Point and Key Lime Pie.

What's one piece of advice you would offer to someone looking to open their own B&B?

Know how to fix toilets and minor plumbing. The scepter with which you rule is a plunger.

What was the hardest part about opening?

The B & B was already open. Hurricanes are stressful, even those that thankfully pass you by.

With the travel industry so competitive, how are you able to find guests? What is your most successful marketing avenue and why do you think that is?

Word of mouth and Tripadvisor and more recently the OTA's. You have to partner with them in this age to be found.

ONE HUNDRED ONE

Brewery Gulch Inn

9401 N. Highway 1
Mendocino, CA 95460

∾

Guy Pacurar
Proprietor

- AAA 4-diamond since 2002

- Consistent recognition in Conde Nast, Travel + Leisure and USA Today top lodging properties in the world lists

- Consistent recipient of TripAdvisor's Travelers' Choice Award

- Member of Green Hotels Association

- Member of Audubon Sanctuary program

WHAT GOT YOU STARTED IN THE **B&B** INDUSTRY?

It is something I have wanted to do since I was a teenager. My family would stay at an apartment hotel in Palm Springs where the owners made everyone feel like part of an extended family.

What is your B&B best known for?

Food and service.

What is your region known for?

Spectacular scenery, lack of crowds, great dining and wine.

What's one piece of advice you would offer to someone looking to open their own B&B?

Take your time looking. I looked at 28 B&Bs from the Northeast to the Southwest before I found the one that resonated with me.

What was the hardest part about opening?

I was lucky in that the inn I purchased had a GM in place. It allowed me to learn as I went with someone in place making sure I didn't mess up too badly.

With the travel industry so competitive, how are you able to find guests?

We are lucky that we have good name recognition and a very high repeat rate for past guests. We don't do any paid advertising, but invest, instead, in a publicist who is very good at what she does.

What is your most successful marketing avenue and why do you think that is?

Creating evangelizers out of our past guests and again, investing in our publicist.

ONE HUNDRED TWO

Market Street Inn

220 E Market St
Taylorville, IL 62568-2212

∽

Myrna & Joe Hauser
Innkeepers for 26 years

NOTES FROM THE INNKEEPERS:

We recently downsized from 10 rooms to only 2 rooms in our carriage house. Our website has been edited to reflect the recent changes. At our age in our late 70's, it is time to slow down. After 26 years of very successful innkeeping, my comments to you are:

Make certain that your website is mobile responsive, so guests can quickly see pics and read reviews. I have heard new guests say that if there are no reviews, then look for an inn with good reviews.

Have your webmaster make on-line reservations available--guests are in a hurry and really don't want to take to innkeeper, especially after reading our great reviews.

We are blessed with strong corporate clientele--garnered by attending monthly Chamber of Commerce social hours, e.g. Had 33 nights of stay when a new shoe store came to town. Our local hospital places temp staff here. Offer flexible breakfast times

Offer free and robust wi-fi----ours is fiber optic. Also place a smart flat screen TV in each guest room.

Our inn was a member of Select Registry for several years--it was mandatory to hand an annual guide book to each guest. It was interesting how several were not interested in a book saying that we do everything on-line. Our Illinois state association has eliminated the guidebook and does everything on-line. With that in mind, I would suggest that you consider on-line offerings as a priority.

ONE HUNDRED THREE

Hawaii's Hidden Hideaway Bed & Breakfast

1369 Mokolea Drive
Kailua, HI 96734

∽

Janice Nielsen

WHAT GOT YOU STARTED IN THE B&B INDUSTRY?

I wanted to provide guests with a local feel of the area and alternative to the high-rise jungle of Waikiki.

What is your B&B best known for?

Hospitality, location, and most of all privacy.

What is your region known for?

> Beautiful white sandy beaches of Lanikai and Kailua, HI

What's one piece of advice you would offer to someone looking to open their own B&B?

> It is a lot of work but rewarding. Also remember that you can't please everyone, and those that are happy rarely write reviews. Be prepared for those that are disgruntled to write bad reviews. I got a one-star rating from someone once, who said the shampoo did not lather enough.

What was the hardest part about opening?

> Getting the word out. We have been in business for more than 20 years, so getting the word out, then was a lot different than it is now.

With the travel industry so competitive, how are you able to find guests?

> We rely upon the internet these days and word of mouth. In days past it was through agents and then internet marketing sites.

What is your most successful marketing avenue and why do you think that is?

> We still use marketing sites, but word of mouth and your own website and getting the word out on social media.

ONE HUNDRED FOUR

Maison de Terre

21704 Uintah Road
Cedaredge CO 81413

∽

Marty and Terrie Watts

What got you started in the B&B industry?

We have a beautiful, unique, adobe home which we build with our own labor. We live in a spectacularly beautiful part of Colorado. As our children have left to pursue their own life adventures, we felt that converting our home not a Bed and Breakfast would allow us to share our home with others as well as supplement our income.

What is your B&B best known for? What is your region known for?

We have a spectacular space, large comfortable hand plastered rooms, stone and adobe floors, hand crafted river rock shower, attached outdoor patio, green house, indoor fish pond, and expansive views of western Colorado. Our breakfasts are culinary delights, fresh lighter than air biscuits with homemade preserves from local fruit, crepes, fresh fruit, local eggs, and extreme friendliness.

As for the area: we are located on the south slope of the Grand Mesa, the worlds largest flat top mountain which is home to over 300 lakes surrounded by spruce, aspen, and pine forests. The mesa affords hiking, hunting, fishing, mountain biking, canoeing, and winter sports (some of the worlds best cross-country skiing and snowmobiling. Going south and visible from our property is the Black Canyon of the Gunnison River National Park, a awe inspiring 2000 foot deep canyon carved into granite cyst over the paste few million years. If that isn't enough, the Gunnison river offers rafting, kayaking, and canoeing adventures ranging from class 4 rapids to peaceful day long float trip in tamer waters the meander through sandstone canyons. Further south one can venture into the San Juan Mountains that afford unforgettable alpine adventures.

What's one piece of advice you would offer to someone looking to open their own B&B?

Be prepared to meet wonderful and diverse people. Serving people is a joy, but it does demand attention to detail and flexibility. We try to tailor our meals to the vast dietary preferences of our guest, requiring a deep reservoir of food options.

What was the hardest part about opening?

Getting adequate insurance was a big obstacle for us, mainly because of our remote location. Also, understanding the state and local regulations is challenging. This has especially been a challenge during the covid-19 pandemic which has been going on for half of the time we have been in business.

With the travel industry so competitive, how are you able to find guests? What is your most successful marketing avenue and why do you think that is?

We have had very little trouble finding guests during the summer months. Our website and reviews show case our place as something special, and people recognize this. We book through Expedia, Airbnb, and our website. Each venue brings a different demographic.

ONE HUNDRED FIVE

Maria's Creekside B&B

2770 E 46th Ave
Anchorage, Alaska 99507

∼

Robert L Bell

- 9.8 out of 10 on Expedia and 9.6 out of 10 on Booking after seven years.

WHAT GOT YOU STARTED IN THE B&B INDUSTRY?

We own a retail store where Maria was our technician for 12 years. One day she said she wanted to open a B&B. I now realize that it was her way of getting out of her comfort zone where meeting people is concerned.

What is your B&B best known for? What is your region known for?

> The common themes with our online reviews is cleanliness and great cooking. Hospitality is actually pretty simple. Keep the place clean and treat people nice. Alaska? Wildlife, Glaciers, and the Aurora.

What's one piece of advice you would offer to someone looking to open their own B&B?

> You need a commercial laundry room. A single washer and dryer is not going to cut it.

What was the hardest part about opening?

> We designed and built our own building. That was nothing compared to setting up the online accounts and channel manager.

With the travel industry so competitive, how are you able to find guests?

> Virtually all guests make their reservation online through Booking.com or one of the Expedia.com sites.

What is your most successful marketing avenue and why do you think that is?

> Booking.com. Their good to us and our guests. I read an article this week that compared Booking and Expedia relative to deposits. Expedia has always taken large deposits. With Covid they had to give back billions. Booking did not. Expedia is now hurting for cash. We have never taken deposits. We did not have to return any deposits with the Covid cancellations.

ONE HUNDRED SIX

Bed and Bagels of Tucson

10402 E Glenn St
Tucson, Arizona 85749

WHAT GOT YOU STARTED IN THE B&B INDUSTRY?

I love to cook and bake and travel and, once I was divorced, had an empty nest and a house of my own with three resident pets, it seemed a natural thing to do.

What is your B&B best known for? What is your region known for?

Friendliness to pets of all sizes and descriptions, elaborate breakfasts, and wealth of knowledge of outdoor and cultural resources in the area. Accommodating to people with chemical sensitivities, children and seniors Tub for kids. Grab bars for seniors. Hot tub and (unheated) pool. Kitchen and laundry privileges

Region (Tucson/southwest Arizona known for great weather in winter, diversity of bird life, lush desert and mountain landscapes, very bike friendly with miles of off-road bikeways great art, theater, and music scene. Numerous craft beer places.

What's one piece of advice you would offer to someone looking to open their own B&B?

Willingness and ability to make total strangers feel at home like old friends.

What was the hardest part about opening?

Letting the world know you exist! I was not very computer savvy when I started, but am good at getting free help.

A young techie guest launched my website in exchange for a few extra free guest days at Bed and Bagels.

With the travel industry so competitive, how are you able to find guests? What is your most successful marketing avenue and why do you think that is?

I tried (and rejected) several marketing avenues: Tucson Convention and Visitors Bureau - was expensive and not productive; ditto for Bedandbreakfast.com (now out of business)

My best source in recent years has been Bringfido.com. I also joined (reluctantly) the Expedia/Travelocity/Hotels.com conglomerate, as well as airbnb in recent years.

I am also listed in the Safer Travel Directory, a guide to accommodations for people with chemical sensitivities. Just by Existing in space, I appear on Google Maps w/o joining or paying anything.

Guests with family or friends in the area find me because I'm close to the people they're visiting.

ONE HUNDRED SEVEN

Black Bear Inn

5528 N Tongass Hwy
Ketchikan, Alaska 99901

∼

Nicole Church

WHAT GOT YOU STARTED IN THE B&B INDUSTRY?

Although neither my husband nor I had ever stayed in a B&B we decided that that might be a great way to meet people from all over the world without leaving Alaska. We owned a piece of property on the ocean in Ketchikan and thought it would be fun to build a small Inn that would attract the kind of guests that we would seek out if we were traveling the world. So we did it.

What is your B&B best known for? What is your region known for?

Personal service, local knowledge, and honest caring friendship.

Fishing and Natures wild life available to all who visit.

What's one piece of advice you would offer to someone looking to open their own B&B?

Things to consider before you start a B&B. There are so many.

Will a B&B in your area really attract the kind of guests you want and be loo able to pay for its self?

Clearly identify your market and decide if you are financially able to Create what is needed.

Do not open one in a home you have lived in long enough where outsiders will feel like an intrusion.

While researching why B&B's failed I learned that many failed because the owners felt to intruded upon.

What was the hardest part about opening?

The hardest part for us was getting all of the building materials and furnishings. We had to buy almost everything in the lower 48 and have it barged to Alaska.

ONE HUNDRED EIGHT

Sweet Dreams B&B

14829 Morrison Street
Sherman Oaks, CA, 91403

∼

Amy Ram
Owner/Innkeeper

- **Official CABBI Associate**

- Top performer on TripAdvisor and have received the TripAdvisor Certificate of Excellence 5 years in a row

WHAT GOT YOU STARTED IN THE B&B INDUSTRY?

As a mother of 4 kids, when they got older and moved out, I was left with quite a bit of space. I truly enjoy being around people and taking care of them. A few friends of mine had decided to start a bed and breakfast and it seemed easy enough.

What is your B&B best known for? What is your region known for?

My B&B is best known for the amazing breakfast spreads that I prepare. Years as a mother gave me the experience necessary to produce a big healthy loving breakfast and create a fun safe space to start the day! Unfortunately, we no longer have breakfast together because of the CoronaVirus Pandemic. I am really looking forward to being able to share stories over breakfast with my guests again!

I am in Los Angeles, California in a region known as "The Valley". The San Fernando Valley is a central suburban area of Los Angeles. Perfect for people who want to be close enough to city life without the noise.

What's one piece of advice you would offer to someone looking to open their own B&B?

Do your research. There has been a surprising increase in government control over the bed and breakfast market. Regulations are now in place that we're not necessary a few years ago.

What was the hardest part about opening?

The hardest part was getting myself advertised. My computer skills are basic and all of the business comes from websites and online! working this B&B has definitely made me more computer savvy.

ONE HUNDRED NINE

Whispering Winds Retreat B&B

65095 Lingonberry Rd
Ninilchik, Alaska 99639

∽

Fred Eggert

For two years in a row, booking.com has recognized us as a highly rated establishment with a customer satisfaction score of 9.7

WHAT GOT YOU STARTED IN THE B&B INDUSTRY?

I wanted to do something different than work for somebody else, and semi-retire in the process. Something that didn't take a huge investment to get going. And a change of scenery helped.

What is your B&B best known for?

Our hospitality, cleanliness, and quiet.

What is your region known for?

World class halibut and salmon fishing.

What's one piece of advice you would offer to someone looking to open their own B&B?

Endeavor to persevere

What was the hardest part about opening?

Getting customers in the door.

With the travel industry so competitive, how are you able to find guests?

Couldn't have done it without internet advertising

What is your most successful marketing avenue and why do you think that is?

Booking engines like expedia.com and booking.com literally reach world wide. We get travelers from everywhere.

ONE HUNDRED TEN

Brigitte's Bavarian Bed und Breakfast

59800 Tern Court, Box 2391
Homer, Alaska 99603

∾

Willie und Brigitte Suter

WHAT GOT YOU STARTED IN THE B&B INDUSTRY?

My Bavarian wife's-parents planned to visit us, spending 6 or so weeks - that was in 1989 - with the Exon oil-spill just happening, we built a small cabin for the parents, our house being far from finished.

After they went back home, we thought of renting the little unit, that went pretty well, Tourism just got *invented* in Alaska. The following year did build onto the cabin, so then had two units to rent. The rooms were built the way the two of us would like to lodge when traveling

What is your B&B best known for? What is your region known for?

Brigitte's Bavarian advertises itself to a specific clientele, ex-military having been stationed over *there* or folks with German blood etc

Homer is know for its beauty etc.

What's one piece of advice you would offer to someone looking to open their own B&B?

Simple and all honest, good quality throughout: service, linen, bed, bathroom, outdoors etc - then food: homemade, own stuff out of the garden, fish, fish, fish - make Sourdough breads etc. Do not cook if you do not like to cook.

What was the hardest part about opening?

One has to have time - new guests are mostly seasoned travelers, word of mouth only goes so far

With the travel industry so competitive, how are you able to find guests? What is your most successful marketing avenue and why do you think that is?

Doing this for some 30 years we still advertise - B&B's are a dime a dozen - Expedia, Booking.com etc. are important to work with

Final Notes

I hope you enjoyed learning about the fabulous B&B's that exist across America. A special thanks goes out to all the businesses that participated and gave up their time and effort to make this possible. If you enjoyed this book then you'll absolutely love the companion book: ***Running a Bed and Breakfast***

| Available Now: Hardcover | Paperback | eBook | Audiobook

Also by Jon Nelsen

- *Starting a Bed and Breakfast: Bite Sized Interviews With Successful B&B's on Building a Brand That Lasts*

- *Running a Bed and Breakfast: Bite Sized Interviews With Successful B&B's on Maintaining a Thriving Inn*

- *One More Beer, Please (Vol. 1, 2, 3): The Largest Collection of Interviews With Brewmasters and Craft Breweries*

- *Solar Panels: Are Solar Panels Worth It?*

- *Complete Guide to Roofing and Solar: Homeowners Essential Handbook for Money Saving DIY Roof Construction and Solar Panels*

- *What I Wish My Roofer Had Told Me: The Ultimate Guide to the Roof of Your Dreams on a Budget*

- *The Only Time I Set the Bar Low Is for Limbo: Reaching Your Potential in Work, Life, and Relationships*

- *What College Didn't Teach You About Getting Hired: The Ultimate Guide on How to Find a Job After Graduation*

- *The Anxiety Answer: The Step-by-Step Guide to Overcoming Fears, Phobias, and Other Voices in Your Head*

- *Solar Powered Energy Theft: Legal No Money Down Solar Panels for Homeowners*

SOLAR POWERED ENERGY THEFT

Why Solar?

- Increase your home's value
- Save up to 50% on monthly energy
- Predictable and fixed cost
- Sell home faster
- Protection from inflation
- Peace of mind

JonNelsen.com
• SOLAR CONSULTANT •

AVAILABLE FREE FOR A LIMITED TIME | *jonnelsen.com*

Made in the USA
Las Vegas, NV
07 June 2024